$$\frac{r_s}{\sqrt{X}} net$$

English Men of Letters

EDITED BY JOHN MORLEY

SIR PHILIP SIDNEY

SIR PHILIP SIDNEY

BY

J. A. SYMONDS

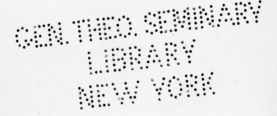

London
MACMILLAN AND CO., Limited
NEW YORK: THE MACMILLAN COMPANY
1906

First Edition 1885
Reprinted 1889, 1902.
1906

PREFACE

THE chief documents upon which a life of Sir Philip Sidney must be grounded are, at present, his own works in prose and verse, Collins' *Sidney Papers* (2 vols., 1745), Sir Henry Sidney's Letter to Sir Francis Walsingham (*Ulster Journal of Archæology*, Nos. 9–31), Languet's *Latin Letters* (Edinburgh, 1776), Pears' *Correspondence of Languet and Philip Sidney* (London, 1845), Fulke Greville's so-called *Life of Sidney* (1652), the anonymous "Life and Death of Sir Philip Sidney," prefixed to old editions of the *Arcadia*, and a considerable mass of memorial writings in prose and verse illustrative of his career. In addition to these sources, which may be called original, we possess a series of modern biographies, each of which deserves mention. These, in their chronological order, are : Dr. Zouch's (1809), Mr. William Gray's (1829), an anonymous *Life and Times of Sir Philip Sidney* (Boston, 1859), Mr. Fox Bourne's (1862), and Mr. Julius Lloyd's (later in 1862). With the American Life I am not acquainted ; but the two last require to be particularly noticed. Mr. Fox Bourne's *Memoir of Sir Philip Sidney* combines a careful study of its main subject with an able review of the times. The author's industrious researches in

State Papers and other MS. collections brought many
new facts to light. This book is one upon which all
later handlings of the subject will be based, and his
deep indebtedness to which every subsequent biographer
of Sidney must recognise. Mr. Lloyd's *Life of Sir
Philip Sidney* appearing in the same year as Mr. Fox
Bourne's, is slighter in substance. It has its own value
as a critical and conscientious study of Sidney under
several aspects; and in one or two particulars it supple-
ments or corrects the more considerable work of Mr.
Bourne. For Sidney's writings Professor Arber's reprint
of the *Defence of Poesy*, and Dr. Grosart's edition of the
poems in two volumes (The Fuller Worthies' Library,
1873), will be found indispensable.

In composing this sketch I have freely availed myself
of all that has been published about Sidney. It has been
my object to present the ascertained facts of his brief
life, and my own opinions regarding his character and
literary works, in as succinct a form as I found
possible.

BADENWEILER, *May* 11, 1886.

CONTENTS

CHAPTER I

PAGE

LINEAGE, BIRTH, AND BOYHOOD 1

CHAPTER II

FOREIGN TRAVEL 20

CHAPTER III

ENTRANCE INTO COURT-LIFE AND EMBASSY . . . 34

CHAPTER IV

THE FRENCH MATCH AND "THE ARCADIA" . . . 64

CHAPTER V

LIFE AT COURT AGAIN, AND MARRIAGE 95

CHAPTER VI

"ASTROPHEL AND STELLA" 115

CONTENTS

CHAPTER VII

PAGE

"The Defence of Poesy" 155

CHAPTER VIII

Last Years and Death 171

INDEX 201

SIR PHILIP SIDNEY

CHAPTER I

LINEAGE, BIRTH, AND BOYHOOD

SHELLEY, in his memorial poem on the death of Keats, named Sir Philip Sidney among "the inheritors of un-fulfilled renown." If this phrase be applicable to Chatterton and Keats, it is certainly, though in a less degree perhaps, true also of Sidney. His best friend and interpreter put on record that "the youth, life, and fortune of this gentleman were, indeed, but sparks of extraordinary greatness in him, which, for want of clear vent, lay concealed, and, in a manner, smothered up." The real difficulty of painting an adequate portrait of Sidney at the present time is that his renown trans-cends his actual achievement. Neither his poetry nor his prose, nor what is known about his action, quite ex-plains the singular celebrity which he enjoyed in his own life, and the fame which has attended his memory with almost undimmed lustre through three centuries. In an age remarkable for the great deeds of its heroes, no less than for the splendour of its literature, he won and retained a homage which was paid to none of his

Œ   B

contemporaries. All classes concurred in worshipping
that marvellous youth, who displayed the choicest gifts
of chivalry and scholarship, of bravery and prudence, of
creative and deliberative genius, in the consummate harmony of a noble character. The English nation seemed
instinctively to recognise in him the impersonation of
its manifold ideals. He was beautiful, and of illustrious
ancestry,—an accomplished courtier, complete in all the
exercises of a cavalier. He was a student, possessed of the
new learning which Italy had recently bequeathed to
Europe. He was a poet and the "warbler of poetic
prose," at a moment when the greater luminaries of the
Elizabethan period had scarcely risen above the horizon.
Yet his beauty did not betray him into levity or wantonness ; his noble blood bred in him neither pride nor
presumption. Courtly habits failed to corrupt his
rectitude of conduct, or to impair the candour of his
utterance. The erudition of the Renaissance left his
Protestant simplicity and Christian faith untouched.
Literary success made him neither jealous nor conceited ;
and as the patron and friend of poets, he was even more
eminent than as a writer. These varied qualities were
so finely blent in his amiable nature that, when Wotton
called him "the very essence of congruity," he hit upon
the happiest phrase for describing Sidney's charm.

The man, in fact, was greater than his words and
actions. His whole life was "a true poem, a composition,
and pattern of the best and honourablest things;" and the
fascination which he exerted over all who came in contact with him—a fascination which extended to those who
only knew him by report—must now, in part at least, be
taken upon trust. We cannot hope to present such a

picture of him as shall wholly justify his fame.   Person-
alities so unique as Sidney's exhale a perfume which
evanesces when the lamp of life burns out.   This the
English nation felt when they put on public mourning for
his death.   They felt that they had lost in Sidney, not
only one of their most hopeful gentlemen and bravest
soldiers, but something rare and beautiful in human life,
which could not be recaptured,—which could not even
be transmitted, save by hearsay, to a future age.   The
living Euphues of that era (so conscious of its aspirations
as yet but partially attained, so apt to idealise its
darlings) had perished—just when all men's eyes were
turned with certainty of expectation on the coming
splendours of his maturity.   "The president of noble-
ness and chivalry" was dead.   "That most heroic spirit,
the heaven's pride, the glory of our days," had passed
away like young Marcellus.   Words failed the survivors
to express their sense of the world's loss.   This they
could not utter, because there was something indescrib-
able, incalculable, in the influence his personality had
exercised.   We, then, who have to deal with meagre records and scanty written remains, must well weigh the
sometimes almost incoherent passion which emerges in
the threnodies poured out upon his grave.   In the grief
of Spenser and of Camden, of Fuller and of Jonson, of
Constable and Nash, of the Countess of Pembroke and
Fulke Greville, as in a glass darkly, we perceive what
magic spell it was that drew the men of his own time to
love and adore Sidney.   The truth is that Sidney, as we
now can know him from his deeds and words, is not an
eminently engaging or profoundly interesting personage.
But, in the mirror of contemporary minds, he shines

with a pure lustre, which the students of his brief
biography must always feel to be surrounding him.

Society, in the sixteenth century, bestowed much in-
genuity upon the invention of appropriate mottoes and
significant emblems.   When, therefore, we read that
Sir Philip Sidney inscribed his shield with these words
Vix ea nostra voco (" These things I hardly call our own "),
we may take it for a sign that he attached no undue
value to noble birth ; and, indeed, he makes one of the
most respectable persons in his *Arcadia* exclaim : " I am
no herald to enquire of men's pedigrees ; it sufficeth me
if I know their virtues." This might justify his biographers in silence regarding his ancestry, were it not
that his connections, both on the father's and the
mother's side, were all-important in determining the
tenor of his life.

The first Sidney of whom we hear anything came into
England with Henry II., and held the office of Chamberlain to that king.   His descendant, Nicholas Sidney,
married a daughter of Sir William Brandon and aunt of
Charles, Duke of Suffolk.   Their son, Sir William Sidney,
played an important part during the reign of Henry VIII. ;
he served in the French wars, and commanded the right
wing of the English army at Flodden.   To him was
given the manor of Penshurst in Kent, which has remained in the possession of the Sidneys and their present
representatives.   On his death in 1554 he left one son
and four daughters.   The eldest of these daughters was
ancestress of Lord Bolingbroke.   From the marriage of
the second to Sir James Harrington descended, by
female alliances, the great house of Montagu and the
families of North and Noel.   Through the marriage of

the third with Sir William Fitz-William, Lord Byron laid claim to a drop of Sidney blood. The fourth, who was the wife of Thomas Ratcliffe, Earl of Sussex, dying childless, founded Sidney Sussex College at Cambridge. With the only son, Sir Henry Sidney (b. 1529-89), we shall have much to do in the present biography. It is enough now to mention that Henry VIII. chose him for bedfellow and companion to his only son. "I was, by that most famous king," he writes, "put to his sweet son, Prince Edward, my most dear master, prince, and sovereign ; my near kinswoman being his only nurse, my father being his chamberlain, my mother his governess, my aunt in such place as among meaner personages is called a dry nurse ; for, from the time he left sucking, she continually lay in bed with him, so long as he remained in women's government. As the prince grew in years and discretion so grew I in favour and liking of him." A portion of Hollingshed's Chronicle, contributed by Edward Molineux, long time Sir Henry Sidney's secretary, confirms this statement. "This right famous, renowned, worthy, virtuous, and heroical knight, by father and mother very nobly descended, was from his infancy bred and brought up in the prince's court and in nearness to his person, used familiarly even as a companion." Nothing but Edward VI.'s untimely death prevented Sir Henry Sidney from rising to high dignity and power in the realm. It was in his arms that the king expired in 1553 at Greenwich.

One year before this event Sir Henry had married the Lady Mary Dudley, daughter of Edmund, Viscount De l'Isle and Duke of Northumberland. The Dudleys were themselves of noble extraction, though one of their

ancestors had perished ignobly on the scaffold. Edmund
Dudley, grandson of John Lord Dudley, K.G., joined
with Sir Richard Empson in those extortions which disgraced the last years of Henry VII.'s reign, and both
were executed in the second year of his successor. His
son, Sir John Dudley, was afterwards relieved of the
attainder, and restored to those honours which he claimed
from his mother. His mother, Elizabeth Grey, was
heiress of a very ancient house, whose baronies and titles
had passed by an almost unexampled series of female
successions. The first founder of the family of De l'Isle
appears in history during the reign of King John. The
last baron of the male blood died in the reign of Richard
II., leaving an heiress, who was married to Thomas Lord
Berkeley. Their daughter and sole heiress married
Richard, Earl of Warwick, and also left an only heiress,
who married John Talbot, the great Earl of Shrewsbury.
Her eldest son, John Talbot, Baron De l'Isle, created
Viscount De l'Isle, left an only daughter, Elizabeth, who
was wedded to Sir Edward Grey, created Baron and
Viscount De l'Isle. It was the daughter and heiress of
this marriage who gave birth to the ambitious and unfortunate Duke of Northumberland. From these dry
facts it will be seen that the descendants of Edmund
Dudley were not only heirs and representatives of the
ancient barony of De l'Isle, but that they also inherited
the blood and arms of the illustrious houses of Berkeley,
Beauchamp, Talbot, and Grey. When we further
remember to what an eminence the Duke of Northumberland climbed, and how his son, the Earl of Leicester, succeeded in restoring the shattered fortunes of the
family after that great prince's fall, we can understand

why Sir Henry Sidney used the following language to
his brother-in-law upon the occasion of Mary Sidney's
betrothal to the Earl of Pembroke :—"I find to my
exceeding great comfort the likelihood of a marriage
between my Lord of Pembroke and my daughter, which
great honour to me, my mean lineage and kin, I attribute
to my match in your noble house." Philip Sidney, too,
when he was called to defend his uncle Leicester against
certain libels, expressed his pride in the connection. "I
am a Dudley in blood; that Duke's daughter's son; and
do acknowledge, though in all truth I may justly affirm
that I am by my father's side of ancient and always well-
esteemed and well-matched gentry,—yet I do acknowledge, I say, that my chiefest honour is to be a Dudley."

Philip was born at Penshurst on the 29th of November 1554. At that epoch their alliance with the Dudleys
seemed more likely to bring ruin on the Sidneys than
new honours. It certainly made their home a house of
mourning. Lady Mary Sidney had recently lost her
father and her brother Guilford on the scaffold. Another
of her brothers, John, Earl of Warwick, after his release
from the Tower, took refuge at Penshurst, and died
there about a month before his nephew's birth.[1] Sir
Henry's loyalty and prudence at this critical time saved
the fortunes of his family. He retired to his country
seat, taking no part in the Duke of Northumberland's
ambitious schemes; and though he was coldly greeted
at Mary's Court, the queen confirmed him in the tenure
of his offices and honours by a deed of 8th November

---

[1] Duke of Northumberland, d. 22d August 1553; Lord Guilford
Dudley and Lady Jane Grey, 12th February 1554; John Dudley,
Earl of Warwick, 21st October 1554.

1554. She also freed his wife from participation in the attainder of her kinsfolk. Their eldest son was christened Philip in compliment to Mary's Spanish consort. It appears that Sir Henry Sidney subsequently gained his sovereign's confidence; for in this reign he was appointed Vice-Treasurer and Controller of the royal revenues in Ireland.

Of Philip's birthplace Ben Jonson has bequeathed to us a description, animated with more of romantic enthusiasm than was common to his muse.

> " Thou art not, Penshurst, built to envious show
> Of touch [1] or marble, nor canst boast a row
> Of polished pillars or a roof of gold :
> Thou hast no lantern, whereof tales are told ;
> Or stair, or courts ; but stand'st an ancient pile ;
> And these, grudged at, are reverenced the while.
> Thou joy'st in better marks, of soil, of air,
> Of wood, of water ; therein art thou fair.
> Thou hast thy walks for health as well as sport :
> Thy mount, to which thy dryads do resort,
> Where Pan and Bacchus their high feasts have made,
> Beneath the broad beech and the chestnut shade ;
> That taller tree, which of a nut was set,
> At his great birth, where all the muses met ;
> There, in the writhed bark, are cut the names
> Of many a Sylvan taken with his flames ;
> And there the ruddy satyrs oft provoke
> The lighter fauns to reach thy lady's oak."

The tree here commemorated by Jonson as having been planted at Sir Philip Sidney's birth, was cut down in 1768, not, however, before it had received additional

---

[1] *Touch* is a superlative sort of marble, the classic *basanites*. The reference to a *lantern* in the next line but one might pass for a prophecy of Walpole's too famous lantern at Houghton.

fame from Edmund Waller. His Sacharissa was the
Lady Dorothea Sidney ; and the poet was paying her
court at Penshurst when he wrote these lines :

> " Go, boy, and carve this passion on the bark
>   Of yonder tree, which stands the sacred mark
>   Of noble Sidney's birth."

Jonson expatiates long over the rural charms of Penshurst, which delighted him on many a summer's holiday.
He celebrates the pastures by the river, the feeding-
grounds of cattle, the well-stocked game preserves, the
fish-ponds, and the deer-park, which supplied that
hospitable board with all good things in season.

> " The painted partridge lies in every field,
>   And for thy mess is willing to be killed ;
>   And if the high-swol'n Medway fail thy dish
>   Thou hast the ponds that pay thee tribute fish,
>   Fat aged carps that run into thy net,
>   And pikes, now weary their own kind to eat,
>   As loth the second draught or cast to stay,
>   Officiously at first themselves betray."

Next he turns to the gardens :—

> " Then hath thy orchard fruit, thy garden flowers,
>   Fresh as the air, and new as are the hours ;
>   The early cherry, with the later plum,
>   Fig, grape, and quince, each in his time doth come ;
>   The blushing apricot and woolly peach,
>   Hang on thy walls, that every child may reach."

The trellised walls remind him of the ancient habita-
tion, which, though homely, is venerable, rearing itself
among the humbler dwellings of the peasants, with
patriarchal rather than despotic dignity.

" And though thy walls be of the country stone,
  They're reared with no man's ruin, no man's groan;
  There's none that dwell about them wish them down,
  But all come in, the farmer and the clown,
  And no one empty-handed to salute
  Thy lord and lady, though they have no suit.
  Some bring a capon, some a rural cake,
  Some nuts, some apples; some that think they make
  The better cheeses, bring them ; or else send
  By their ripe daughters, whom they would commend
  This way to husbands, and whose baskets bear
  An emblem of themselves in plum or pear."

This poem, composed in the days when Philip's
brother, Sir Robert Sidney, was master of Penshurst,
presents so charming a picture of the old-world home in
which Philip was born, and where he passed his boyhood, that I have been fain to linger over it.

Sir Henry Sidney was sent to Ireland in 1556 as
Vice-Treasurer and General Governor of the royal revenues in that kingdom.   He distinguished himself,
soon after his arrival, by repelling an invasion of the
Scots in Ulster, and killing James MacConnel, one of
their leaders, with his own hand.   Next year he was
nominated Lord Justice of Ireland ; and, on the accession
of Queen Elizabeth, he obtained the confirmation of his
offices.   In 1558 the queen nominated him Lord President of Wales, which dignity he held during the rest of
his life.   It does not exactly appear when he first took
the rank of Lord Deputy of Ireland, a title corresponding
to that of Lord Lieutenant.   But throughout the first
seven years of Elizabeth's reign he discharged functions
there which were equivalent to the supreme command.
In 1564 he received the honour of the Garter, being in-

stalled in the same election with King Charles IX. of
France. On this occasion he was styled "The thrice
valiant Knight, Deputy of the Realm of Ireland, and
President of the Council of Wales." Next year he was
again despatched to Ireland with the full title and
authority of Lord Deputy.

The administration of Wales obliged Sir Henry
Sidney to reside frequently at Ludlow Castle, and
this was the reason which determined him to send
Philip to school at Shrewsbury. Being the emporium
of English commerce with North Wales and Ireland, and the centre of a thriving wool-trade, Shrewsbury had then become a city of importance. The
burgesses established there a public school, which
flourished under the able direction of Thomas Ashton.
From a passage in Ben Jonson's prose works it is clear
that the advantages of public school education were well
appreciated at that time in England. Writing to a
nobleman, who asked him how he might best train up
his sons, he says : "I wish them sent to the best school,
and a public. They are in more danger in your own
family among ill servants than amongst a thousand boys,
however immodest. To breed them at home is to breed
them in a shade, whereas in a school they have the light
and heat of the sun. They are used and accustomed to
things and men. When they come forth into the
commonwealth, they find nothing new or to seek. They
have made their friendships and aids, some to last till
their age." One such friend, whose loving help was
given to Sidney till death parted them, entered Shrewsbury school together with him on the 19th of November
1574. This was Fulke Greville, a distant relative, and

a boy of exactly the same age. To the sincere attach-
ment which sprang up between them, and strengthened
with their growing age, we owe our most valuable inform-
ation regarding Philip's character and opinions. Fulke
Greville survived his friend, became Lord Brooke, and
when he died in 1628 the words "Friend to Philip
Sidney" were inscribed upon his tomb. From the
short biography of his friend, prefixed to a collection
of his own works, which was dedicated to Sidney's
memory, we obtain a glimpse of the boy while yet
at school :—

" Of his youth I will report no other wonder but this,
that though I lived with him, and knew him from a child,
yet I never knew him other than a man ; with such staid-
ness of mind, lovely and familiar gravity as carried grace
and reverence above greater years. His talk ever of knowledge, and his very play tending to enrich his mind. So as
even his teachers found something to observe and learn
above that which they had usually read or taught. Which
eminence, by nature and industry, made his worthy father
style Sir Philip in my hearing (though I unseen) *Lumen
familiæ suæ.*"

According to our present notions, we do not consider it
altogether well if a boy between the ages of ten and fifteen
wins praise for exceptional gravity. Yet Fulke Greville
does not call Philip bookish ; and we have abundant
evidence that, while he was early heedful of nourishing
his mind, he showed no less eagerness to train his body
in such exercises as might be serviceable to a gentleman,
and useful to a soldier. Nevertheless, his friend's ad-
miring eulogy of the lad's deportment indicates what, to
the end, remained somewhat chilling in his nature—a
certain stiffness, want of impulse—want, perhaps, of salu-

tary humour. He could not take the world lightly—
could not act, except in rare moments of anger, without
reflection. Such a character is admirable; and youths
at our public schools, who remain overgrown boys in
their games until they verge on twenty, might well take
a leaf from Sidney's book. But we cannot refrain
from thinking that just a touch of recklessness would
have made him more attractive. We must, however,
remember that he was no child of the nineteenth
century. He belonged to the age of Burleigh and of
Bacon, and the circumstances of his birth forced on him
precocity in prudence. Being the heir of Sir Henry
Sidney and Lady Mary Dudley, he could not but be
early conscious of the serious difficulties which perplexed
his parents. Had he not been also conscious of a calling
to high things, he would have derogated from his illustrious lineage. His gravity, then, befitted his blood and
position in that still feudal epoch, his father's eminent
but insecure station, and the tragic fate of his maternal
relatives.

A letter written by Sir Henry Sidney to his son,
while still at school in Shrewsbury, may here be
cited. It helps to show why Philip, even as a boy, was
earnest. Sympathetic to his parents, bearing them sincere love, and owing them filial obedience, he doubtless
read with veneration, and observed with loyalty, the
words of wisdom—wiser than those with which Polonius
took farewell of Laertes—dictated for him by the up-
right and valiant man whom he called father. Long as
it is, I shall give it in full; for nothing could better
bring before our eyes the ideal of conduct which then
ruled English gentlefolk :—

"I have received two letters from you, one written in Latin, the other in French; which I take in good part, and wish you to exercise that practice of learning often; for that will stand you in most stead in that profession of life that you are born to live in. And since this is my first letter that ever I did write to you, I will not that it be all empty of some advices, which my natural care for you provoketh me to wish you to follow, as documents to you in this your tender age. Let your first action be the lifting up of your mind to Almighty God by hearty prayer; and feelingly digest the words you speak in prayer, with continual meditation and thinking of Him to whom you pray and of the matter for which you pray. And use this as an ordinary act, and at an ordinary hour, whereby the time itself shall put you in remembrance to do that which you are accustomed to do in that time. Apply your study to such hours as your discreet master doth assign you, earnestly; and the time I know he will so limit as shall be both sufficient for your learning and safe for your health. And mark the sense and the matter of that you read, as well as the words. So shall you both enrich your tongue with words and your wit with matter; and judgment will grow as years groweth in you. Be humble and obedient to your master, for unless you frame yourself to obey others, yea, and feel in yourself what obedience is, you shall never be able to teach others how to obey you. Be courteous of gesture and affable to all men, with diversity of reverence according to the dignity of the person: there is nothing that winneth so much with so little cost. Use moderate diet, so as after your meal you may find your wit fresher and not duller, and your body more lively and not more heavy. Seldom drink wine, and yet sometimes do, lest being enforced to drink upon the sudden you should find yourself inflamed. Use exercise of body, yet such as is without peril of your joints or bones; it will increase your force and enlarge your breath. Delight to be cleanly, as well in all parts of your body as in your garments: it shall make you grateful in each company, and otherwise loathsome. Give yourself to be merry, for you degenerate from your father if you find not yourself most able in wit and body and to do anything when you be most merry; but let your mirth be ever void of all scurrility and biting words to any man, for a wound given by a word is oftentimes harder to be cured than that which is given with the sword. Be you rather a hearer and bearer away of other men's talk than a beginner and procurer of speech; otherwise you shall be counted to delight to hear yourself speak. If you hear a wise sentence or an apt phrase commit it to your memory with respect of the circumstance when you shall speak it. Let never oath be heard to come out of your mouth nor word of ribaldry; detest it in others; so shall custom make to yourself a law against it in yourself. Be modest in each assembly; and rather be rebuked of light fellows for maiden-like shamefastness than of your sad friends for pert boldness. Think upon every word that you will speak before you utter it, and remember how nature hath ramparted up, as it were, the tongue with teeth, lips, yea, and hair without the lips, and all betokening reins or bridles for the loose use of that member. Above all things, tell no untruth; no, not in trifles: the custom of it is naughty. And let it not satisfy you that, for a time, the hearers take it for truth; for after it will be known as it is, to your shame; for there cannot be a greater reproach to a gentleman than to be accounted a liar. Study and endeavour yourself to be virtuously occupied, so shall you make such a habit of well-doing in you that you shall not know how to do evil, though you would. Remember, my son, the noble blood you are descended of, by your mother's side; and think that only by virtuous life and good action you may be an ornament to that illustrious family, and otherwise, through vice and sloth you shall be counted *labes generis,* one of the greatest curses that can happen to man. Well, my little Philip, this is enough for me, and too much, I fear, for you. But if I shall find that this light meal of digestion nourisheth anything in the weak stomach of your capacity, I will, as I find the same grow stronger, feed it with tougher food.—Your loving father, so long as you live in the fear of God,   H. SIDNEY."

To this epistle Lady Mary Sidney added a postscript, which, if it is less correct in style and weighty with

wise counsel, interests us by its warm and motherly
affection.

"Your noble and careful father hath taken pains (with his
own hand) to give you in this his letter so wise, so learned,
and most requisite precepts for you to follow with a diligent
and humble thankful mind, as I will not withdraw your eyes
from beholding and reverent honouring the same,—no, not
so long time as to read any letter from me; and therefore at
this time I will write no other letter than this: and hereby
I first bless you with my desire to God to plant in you His
grace, and secondarily warn you to have always before the
eyes of your mind those excellent counsels of my lord, your
dear father, and that you fail not continually once in four or
five days to read them over. And for a final leave-taking
for this time, see that you show yourself a loving obedient
scholar to your good master, and that my lord and I may
hear that you profit so in your learning as thereby you may
increase our loving care of you, and deserve at his hands the
continuance of his great joys, to have him often witness with
his own hand the hope he hath in your well-doing.

"Farewell, my little Philip, and once again the Lord bless
you.—Your loving mother,   MARY SIDNEY."

In those days boys did not wait till they were grown
men before they went to college. Sidney left Shrewsbury in 1568, and began residence at Christ Church.
He was still in his fourteenth year. There he stayed
until some time in 1571, when he quitted Oxford without
having taken a degree. In this omission there was
nothing singular. His quality rendered bachelorship or
mastership of arts indifferent to him; and academical
habits were then far freer than in our times. That he
studied diligently is, however, certain. The unknown
writer named Philophilippus, who prefixed a short essay
on "The Life and Death of Sir Philip Sidney" to the
Arcadia, speaks thus in his quaint language of the years

spent at Oxford : "Here an excellent stock met with the choicest grafts ; nor could his tutors pour in so fast as he was ready to receive." The Dean of Christ Church, Dr. Thomas Thornton, had it afterwards engraved upon his own tomb at Ledbury that he had been the preceptor of "Philip Sidney, that most noble Knight." We possess few particulars which throw any light upon Sidney's academical career. There is some reason, however, to believe that liberal learning at this period flourished less upon the banks of the Isis than at Cambridge and in our public schools. Bruno, in his account of a visit to Oxford ten years later, introduces us to a set of pompous pedants, steeped in mediæval scholasticism and heavy with the indolence of fat fellowships. Here, however, Sidney made the second great friendship of his youth. It was with Edward Dyer, a man of quality and parts, who claims distinction as an English poet principally by one faultless line : "My mind to me a kingdom is." Sir Edward Dyer and Sir Fulke Greville lived in bonds of closest affection with Sir Philip Sidney through his life, and walked together as pall-bearers at his funeral. That was an age in which friendship easily assumed the accents of passionate love. I may use this occasion to quote verses which Sidney wrote at a later period regarding his two comrades. He had recently returned from Wilton to the Court, and found there both Greville and Dyer.

> " My two and I be met,
> A blessed happy trinity,
>   As three most jointly set
> In firmest bond of unity.
>   Join hearts and hands, so let it be ;
>   Make but one mind in bodies three.

C

> " Welcome my two to me,
> The number best beloved;
>   Within the heart you be
> In friendship unremoved.
>   Join hearts and hands, so let it be;
>   Make but one mind in bodies three."

And again, when tired of the Court, and sighing for the country, he offers up a prayer to Pan, according to the pastoral fashion of the age, in which his two heart's brothers are remembered :—

> " Only for my two loves' sake,
> In whose love I pleasure take;
> Only two do me delight
> With their ever-pleasing sight;
> Of all men to thee retaining
> Grant me with those two remaining."

As poetry these pieces are scarcely worth citation. But they agreeably illustrate their author's capacity for friendship.

It was also from Oxford that Sidney sent the first letter still extant in his writing. This is a somewhat laboured Latin epistle to his uncle Leicester. Elizabeth's favourite had taken his nephew under special protection. It was indeed commonly accepted for certain that, failing legitimate issue, the Earl intended to make Philip his heir. This expectation helps us to understand the singular respect paid him through these years of early manhood. Sir Henry Sidney was far from being a rich man. His duties in Ireland and Wales removed him from the circle of the Court, and his bluntness of speech made him unacceptable to the queen. Philip therefore owed more of his prestige to his uncle than to his father.

At this time Leicester appears to have been negotiating a marriage contract between the lad at Christ Church and Anne Cecil, daughter of Lord Burleigh. Articles had been drawn up. But the matter fell through; the powerful Secretary of State judging that he could make a better match for his girl than with the son of a needy knight, whose expectations of succeeding to Leicester's estate were problematical. Politely but plainly he extricated himself from the engagement, and bestowed Anne upon Edward de Vere, the dissolute and brutal Earl of Oxford. This passage in the life of Sidney is insignificant. That the boy of sixteen could have entertained any strong feeling for his projected bride will hardly admit of belief. One of his biographers, however, notices that about the time when the matter terminated in Anne's betrothal to the Earl of Oxford, Philip fell into bad health. Leicester had to obtain permisson for him to eat flesh in Lent from no less a personage than Doctor Parker, the Archbishop of Canterbury.

CHAPTER II

It is not the business of Sir Philip Sidney's biographer to discuss Elizabeth's Irish policy at length. Yet his father's position as governor of the island renders some allusion to those affairs indispensable. Sir Henry Sidney was a brave and eminently honest man, the sturdy servant of his sovereign, active in the discharge of his duties, and untainted by corrupt practice. But he cannot be said to have displayed the sagacity of genius in his dealings with the Irish. He carried out instructions like a blunt proconsul—extirpating O'Neil's rebellion, suppressing the Butlers' war, maintaining English interests, and exercising impartial justice. The purity of his administration is beyond all doubt. Instead of enriching himself by arts familiar to viceroys, he spent in each year of his office more than its emoluments were worth, and seriously compromised his private fortune. Instead of making friends at Court he contrived, by his straightforward dealing, to offend the brilliant and subtle Earl of Ormond. While Sir Henry was losing health, money, and the delights of life among the bogs and wastes of Ulster, Ormond remained attached to the queen's person. His beauty and adroit flattery

enabled him to prejudice Elizabeth against her faithful
henchman. Broken in health by a painful disease contracted in the hardship of successive campaigns, mad-
dened by his sovereign's recriminations, and disgusted
by her parsimony, Sir Henry Sidney returned in 1571
to England. He was now a man of forty-three, with an
impaired constitution and a diminished estate. His
wife had lost her good looks in the small-pox, which she
caught while nursing the queen through an attack of
that malady. Of this noble lady, so patient in the many
disasters of her troubled life, Fulke Greville writes : "She
chose rather to hide herself from the curious eyes of a
delicate time than come upon the stage of the world
with any manner of disparagement ; this mischance of
sickness having cast such a veil over her excellent
beauty as the modesty of that sex doth many times
upon their native and heroical spirits." Neither Sir
Henry Sidney nor Lady Mary uttered a word of reproach
against their royal mistress. It was Elizabeth's good
fortune to be devotedly served by men and women whom
she rewarded with ingratitude or niggardly recognition.
And on this occasion she removed Sir Henry from his
dignity of Lord Deputy, which she transferred to his
brother-in-law, Sir William Fitz-William. As a kind of
recompense she made him the barren offer of a peerage.
The distinction was great, but the Sidneys were not in
a position to accept it. A letter, addressed to Lady
Mary by Lord Burleigh, explains the difficulty in which
they stood. Her husband, she says, is "greatly dis-
mayed with his hard choice, which is presently offered
him ; as, either to be a baron, now called in the number
of many far more able than himself to maintain it

withal, or else, in refusing it, to incur her Highness's
displeasure." She points out that the title, without an
accompanying grant of land, would be an intolerable
burden. Elizabeth had clearly no intention of bestowing
estates on the Sidney family; and Lady Mary was
forced to beg the secretary's good offices for mitigating
the royal anger in the event of Sir Henry's refusal.
Of the peerage we hear no more; and it is probable that
Elizabeth took the refusal kindly. She had paid the late
Deputy for his long service and heavy losses by a compliment, his non-acceptation of which left her with a
seat in the House of Lords at her disposal.

After leaving Oxford, Philip passed some months at
Ludlow with his father, who continued to be President
of Wales. In the spring of 1572 the project of a
French match was taken up at Court. Mr. Francis
Walsingham, the resident ambassador at Paris, had
already opened negotiations on the subject in the pre-
vious autumn; and the execution of the Duke of
Norfolk for treasonable practice with Mary, Queen of
Scots, now rendered Elizabeth's marriage more than ever
politically advisable. It was to be regretted that the
queen should meditate union with the Duke of Alençon.
He was the youngest member of the worthless family of
Valois, a Papist, and a man green in years enough to be
her son. Yet at this epoch it seemed not wholly impossible that France might still side with the Protestant
Powers. Catherine de' Medici, the queen mother, had
favoured the Huguenot party for some years; and
Charles IX. was scheming the marriage of his sister
Margaret with Henry of Navarre. The interests, moreover, of the French Crown were decidedly opposed to

those of Spain. The Earl of Lincoln was, therefore, nominated Ambassador Extraordinary to sound the matter of his queen's contract with a prince of the French blood-royal. Sir Henry Sidney seized this opportunity for sending Philip on the grand tour; and Elizabeth granted licence to "her trusty and well-beloved Philip Sidney, Esq., to go out of England into parts beyond the sea, with three servants and four horses, etc., to remain the space of two years immediately following his departure out of the realm, for the attaining the knowledge of foreign languages." On the 26th of May the expedition left London, Philip carrying a letter from his uncle Leicester to Francis Walsingham. This excellent man, who was destined after some years to become his father-in-law, counted among the best and wisest of English statesmen. He was a man of Sir Henry Sidney's, rather than of Leicester's, stamp; and it is recorded of him, to his honour, that, after a life spent in public service, he died so poor that his funeral had to be conducted at night.

When Lincoln returned to England with advice in favour of Alençon's suit, Philip stayed at Paris. The summer of 1572 was an eventful one in French history. Charles IX. had betrothed his sister, Margaret of Valois, to Henry of Navarre; and the Capital welcomed Catholic and Huguenot nobles, the flower of both parties which divided France, on terms of external courtesy and seeming friendship. Fulke Greville tells us that the king of Navarre was so struck with Philip's excellent disposition that he admitted him to intimacy. At the same time Charles IX., who had been installed Knight of the Garter on the same day as Philip's father, appointed him

Gentleman in Ordinary of his bedchamber. The patent runs as follows : "That considering how great the house of Sidenay was in England, and the rank it had always held near the persons of the kings and queens, their sovereigns, and desiring well and favourably to treat the young Sir Philip Sidenay for the good and commendable knowledge in him, he had retained and received him," etc. On the 9th of August "Baron Sidenay," as he is also described in this document, took the oaths and entered on his new office. His position at the French Court made him to some extent an actor in the ceremonial of Henry's wedding, which took place upon the 18th of August. It will be remembered that Margaret of Navarre had previously been pledged to the Duke of Guise, the ambitious leader of the League, the sworn enemy to Reform, and the almost openly avowed aspirant after the French Crown. Before the altar she refused to speak or bend her head, when asked if she accepted Henry for her husband ; and her brother had to take her by the neck and force her into an attitude of assent. Already, then, upon the nuptial morning, ominous clouds began to gather over the political horizon. When the Duke of Guise marched his armed bands into Paris, the situation grew hazardous for the Huguenots. Then followed the attack upon Coligny's life, which exploded like the first cannon shot that preludes a general engagement. Yet the vain rejoicings in celebration of that ill-omened marriage continued for some days ; until, when all was ready, on the 24th of August, Paris swam with the blood of Huguenots. Anarchy and murder spread from the Capital to the provinces ; and during the seven days and more which followed, it is not known how many thousands of Protestants perished. In Rome *Te Deums* were sung, and commemorative medals struck. In England the Court went into mourning. The French ambassador, when ordered by his master to explain the reasons of the Massacre of St. Bartholomew to Elizabeth, excused himself from the performance of this duty. His words deserve to be recorded : "I should make myself an accomplice in that terrible business were I to attempt to palliate." The same man has also left a vivid account of his reception at Woodstock when the news arrived. "A gloomy sorrow sat on every face. Silence, as in the dead of night, reigned through all the chambers of the royal apartments. The ladies and courtiers were ranged on each side, all clad in deep mourning ; and as I passed them, not one bestowed on me a civil look or made the least return of my salutes."

Philip had taken refuge at the English embassy, and to this circumstance he possibly owed his life. The horrors of St. Bartholomew must, however, have made a terrible impression on his mind ; for there was no street in Paris which did not resound with the shrieks of the assassinated, the curses of their butchers, and the sharp ring of musketry. He knew that the king, intoxicated with a sudden blood-thirst, had levelled his harquebuss from that window in the Louvre ; he knew that the Duke of Guise had trampled with his heel upon Coligny's naked corpse. It cannot be doubted that the bold and firm opposition which Philip subsequently offered to Elizabeth's French schemes of marriage had its root in the awful experience of those days of carnage.

Early in September Lords Leicester and Burleigh despatched a formal letter from the Privy Council to

Francis Walsingham, requesting him to provide for the safety of young Lord Wharton and Master Philip Sidney by procuring passports in due form, and sending them immediately back to England. It seems, however, that Sir Henry Sidney did not think a return to England necessary in his son's case. Philip left Paris, passed through Lorraine, visited Strasburg, stopped at Heidelberg, and came thence to Frankfort.

It would be interesting to know what social and political impressions the young man, now in his eighteenth year, carried away with him from Paris. Had he learned the essential baseness and phlegmatic wickedness of the Florentine queen-mother? Had he discerned that the king, crazy, misled, and delirious in his freaks and impulses, was yet the truest man of all his miserable breed? Had he taken a right measure of the Duke of Anjou—ghastly, womanish, the phantom of a tyrant; oscillating between Neronian debauchery and hysterical relapses into pietism? And the Duke of Alençon, Elizabeth's frog-faced suitor, had he perceived in him the would-be murderer of his brother, the poisonous traitor, whose innate malignancy justified his sister Margaret in saying that, if fraud and cruelty were banished from the world, he alone would suffice to re-people it with devils? Probably not; for the backward eye of the historian is more penetrative into the realities of character than the broad, clear gaze of a hopeful gentleman upon his travels. We sound the depths revealed to us by centuries of laborious investigation. He only beheld the brilliant, the dramatic, the bewilderingly fantastic outside of French society, as this was displayed in nuptial pomps and tournaments and

massacres before him.   Yet he observed enough to make
him a firmer patriot a more determined Protestant, and
an abhorrer of Italianated Courts.   At Frankfort he
found a friend, who, having shared the perils of St.
Bartholomew, had recently escaped across the Rhine to
Germany.   This was Hubert Languet, a man whose
conversation and correspondence exercised no small influence over the formation of Sidney's character.

Languet was a Frenchman, born in 1518 at Viteaux
in Burgundy.   He studied the humanities in Italy, and
was elected Professor of Civil Law at Padua in 1547.
Two years later he made the acquaintance of Melanchthon.
Their intercourse ripened into friendship.   Languet
resigned his professorship in order to be near the man
whom he had chosen for his teacher; and under Melanchthon's influence he adopted the reformed religion.   From
1550 forwards he was recognised as one of the leading
political agents of the Protestant Powers, trusted by
princes, and acquainted with the ablest men of that
party in France, Holland, and the German States.   No
one was more competent to guide Sidney through the
labyrinth of European intrigues, to unmask the corruption hidden beneath the splendours of the Valois Court,
and to instil into his mind those principles of conduct
which governed reformed statesmen in those troubled
times.   They were both staying, as was then the custom,
in the house of the printer Wechel at Frankfort.   A few
years later, Giordano Bruno also sojourned under that
hospitable roof, whence he departed on his fatal journey
to Venice.   The elder man immediately discerned in
Sidney a youth of no common quality, and the attach-
ment he conceived for him savoured of romance.   We

possess a long series of Latin letters from Languet to his friend, which breathe the tenderest spirit of affection, mingled with wise counsel and ever-watchful thought for the young man's higher interests. It was indeed one of Sidney's singular felicities that he fell so early under the influence of characters like Walsingham and Languet. Together with his father, they helped to correct the bias which he might have taken from his brilliant but untrustworthy uncle Leicester. There must have been something inexplicably attractive in his person and his genius at this time ; for the tone of Languet's corre-spondence can only be matched by that of Shakespeare in the sonnets written for his unknown friend.

Fulke Greville has penned a beautiful description of " this harmony of an humble hearer to an excellent teacher," which grew up between Sidney and Languet at Frankfort ; but he is mistaken in saying that the latter threw up all other business for the sake of attend-ing his new-found friend upon his three years' travel. It is true that they went together to Vienna in the summer of 1573. But Sidney visited Hungary alone, and in November crossed the Alps without Languet to Venice. He was accompanied by a gentleman of his own age and station, not very distantly connected with him, named Thomas Coningsby. Two of his attendants, Griffin Madox and Lewis Brysket, are also known to us. The latter writes thus of their journey :

> " Through many a hill and dale,
> Through pleasant woods, and many an unknown way,
> Along the banks of many silver streams
> Thou with him yodest ; and with him didst scale
> The craggy rocks of the Alps and Apennine ;
> Still with the muses sporting."

One incident of the tour has to be recorded for the light it throws on Sidney's character. An innkeeper contrived to get his bill twice paid ; and Sidney finding himself out of pocket, charged Coningsby with having made away with the money. In a letter to Languet he cleared the matter up, and exculpated his travelling companion. But the incident was not greatly to his credit. With all his gravity and suavity of nature, he was apt to yield to temper and to unamiable suspicion. I shall have to revert to this point again.

Since Sidney is now launched, without guide or tutor, upon his Italian travels, it will not be out of place to collect some contemporary opinions regarding the benefit to be derived by Englishmen from Italy. In a fine passage of "The Schoolmaster" Ascham relates a conversation which he had at Windsor with Sir Richard Sackville on this subject. His judgment was that young men lost far more than they gained by an Italian tour. Too many of them returned Papists, or Atheists, experienced in newfangled vices, apt for treason, lying, and every form of swinish debauchery. Taking for his text the well-known proverb, "*Inglese italianato è un diavolo incarnato*,"—which Sidney, by the way, has translated thus :

> " An Englishman that is Italianate,
>   Doth lightly prove a devil incarnate,"—

Ascham preaches an eloqent sermon, with allegories from Plato and Homer, to prove that Italy is but a garden of Circe or an isle of sirens to our northern youth. Parker, Howell, Fuller, Hall, Gabriel Harvey, Marston, Greene, all utter the same note, and use the

same admonishments, proving how very dangerous an
Italian tour was reckoned in those days. Sidney, in a
remarkable letter to Languet, insists upon the point.
He says he wishes the Turks could come to Italy in order
to find corruption there : "I am quite sure that this
ruinous Italy would so poison the Turks themselves,
would so ensnare them in its vile allurements, that they
would soon tumble down without being pushed." Venice,
in particular, had an evil reputation. There, as Ascham
says, he saw in nine days' sojourn "more liberty to sin
than ever I heard tell of in our noble city of London in
nine years." He admits, however, that while he knows
of many who "returned out of Italy worse transformed
than ever was any in Circe's court," yet is he acquainted
with "divers noble personages and many worthy gentlemen of England, whom all the siren songs of Italy could
never untwine from the mast of God's word, nor no
enchantment of vanity overturn them from the fear of
God and love of honesty." To the former class belonged
the Earl of Oxford. Of the latter Philip Sidney was
an eminent example. Like the bee which sucks honey
from poisonous flowers, he gained only good from the
travels which were so pernicious to his fellow-country-
men at large.

His correspondence with Languet was doubtless useful to him, while residing at Venice and Padua.
From it we learn something about his studies, which
seem at this time to have been chiefly in philosophy
and science. Languet urges him not to overwork
himself ; and he replies: "I am never so little troubled
with melancholy as when my mind is employed about
something particularly difficult." Languet on another

occasion dissuades him from geometry : " You have too little mirthfulness in your nature, and this is a study which will make you still more grave." He recommends him to devote his time to such things as befit a man of high rank in life, and to prepare himself for the duties of a statesman rather than for the leisure of a literary man. Sidney begs for a copy of Plutarch in Amyot's translation, says he is " learning astronomy and getting a knowledge of music," and is anxious to read the Politics of Aristotle. Meanwhile he frequented the sumptuous houses of the Venetian nobles : " Yet I would rather have one pleasant chat with you, my dear Languet, than enjoy all the magnificent magnificences of these magnificoes." He seems indeed to have been a grave youth. Who his intimate friends were, we do not know. Sarpi was away at Mantua ; so it is not likely that he made his acquaintance. We hear, however, much of the young Count Philip Lewis of Hannau.

At Venice Sidney sat for his portrait to Paolo Veronese, and sent the picture afterwards to Languet. What has become of this painting is not known. Possibly it still lies buried in some German collection. Of all the portraits which are supposed to represent Sidney, the best to my mind is one now preserved at Warwick Castle. It is said to have belonged to Fulke Greville, and therefore we may trust its resemblance to the original. John Aubrey, the useful anecdote-monger, tells us that he was " extremely beautiful. He much resembled his sister ; but his hair was not red, but a little inclining, namely a dark amber colour. If I were to find a fault in it, methinks 'tis not masculine enough; yet he was a person of great courage." The Warwick Castle portrait answers

very closely to this description, especially in a certain almost girlish delicacy of feature and complexion. That
Sidney was indeed beautiful may be taken for granted,
since there is considerable concurrence of testimony on
this point. The only dissentient I can call to mind is
Ben Jonson, who reported that he "was no pleasant
man in countenance, his face being spoiled with pimples,
and of high blood, and long." But Jonson was only
thirteen years of age when Sidney died, and the con-
versations with Drummond, from which this sentence is
quoted, abound in somewhat random statements.

It was natural that a Telemachus of Sidney's stamp
should wish to visit Rome before he turned his face north-
wards. But his Huguenot Mentor, and perhaps also his
friends at home, so urgently dissuaded him from exposing
his immaturity to the blandishments of the Catholic
Calypso, that he prudently refrained. After a short
excursion to Genoa, he returned to Venice, crossed the
Alps, and was again with Languet at Vienna in July.
Here the grave youth, who had set his heart on becoming perfect in all gentle accomplishments, divided his
time between discourse on politics and literature, courtly
pleasures, and equestrian exercises. In the *Defence
of Poesy* he has given us an agreeable picture of
his Italian master in horsemanship, the gasconading
Pugliano.

The winter of 1574-75 passed away at Vienna. In
the spring he attended the Emperor Maximilian to
Prague, where he witnessed the opening of the Bohemian
Diet. Thence he moved homewards through Dresden,
Heidelberg, Strasburg, and Frankfort, reaching London
in June. During his absence one of his two sisters,

Ambrozia, had died at Ludlow Castle. The queen took the other, Mary, under special protection, and attached her to her person. A new chapter was now opened in the young man's life. His education being finished, he entered upon the life of Courts.

CHAPTER III

SIDNEY'S prospects as a courtier were excellent. His powerful uncle Leicester, now at the height of royal favour, displayed marked partiality for the handsome youth, who was not unnaturally regarded by the world as his presumptive heir. In July 1575 Philip shared those famous festivities with which the earl entertained Elizabeth at Kenilworth; and when the Court resumed its progress, he attended her Majesty to Chartley Castle. This was the seat of the Earl of Essex, who was then in Ireland. The countess, in his absence, received her royal guest; and here Sidney, for the first time, met the girl with whom his fortunes and his fame were destined to be blended. Lady Penelope Devereux, illustrious in English literature as Sir Philip Sidney's Stella, was now in her thirteenth year; and it is not likely that at this time she made any strong impression on his fancy. Yet we find that soon after the return of Essex from Ireland in the autumn of 1575, he had become intimate with the earl's family. At Durham House, their London residence, he passed long hours during the following winter; and when Essex went again to Ireland as Earl-Marshal in July 1576, Philip accompanied him. It should here be said that Sir Henry Sidney had been nominated for the third time Lord Deputy in August 1575. Philip's visit was therefore paid to his father; but he made it in company with the man whom he had now come to regard as his future father-in-law. There is little doubt that had Lord Essex lived, the match would have been completed. But the Earl-Marshal died at Dublin on the 21st of September, after a painful illness, which raised some apparently ill-founded suspicions of poison. Philip was in Galway with his father, and Essex sent him this message on his deathbed : " Tell him I sent him nothing, but I wish him well; so well that, if God do move their hearts, I wish that he might match with my daughter. I call him son; he is so wise, virtuous, and godly. If he go on in the course he hath begun, he will be as famous and worthy a gentleman as ever England bred." These words are sufficient to prove that Philip's marriage with Penelope was contemplated by her father. That the world expected it appears from a letter of Mr. Edward Waterhouse to Sir Henry Sidney under date 14th November. After first touching upon the bright prospects opened for "the little Earl of Essex," this gentleman proceeds : "and I suppose all the best sort of the English lords, besides, do expect what will become of the treaty between Mr Philip and my Lady Penelope. Truly, my Lord, I must say to your Lordship, as I have said to my Lord of Leicester and Mr. Philip, the breaking off from their match, if the default be on your parts, will turn to more dishonour than can be repaired with any other marriage in England."

What interrupted the execution of this marriage treaty is not certain. Penelope's mother, the widowed Lady Essex, was privately wedded to the Earl of Leicester soon after her first husband's death. The Sidneys were poor. Lady Mary Sidney writes to Lord Burleigh about this time : " My present estate is such by reason of my debts, as I cannot go forward with any honourable course of living." It is remarkable that, so far as we know, she placed but little confidence in her brother Leicester, preferring to appeal in difficulties to a friend like Cecil. Philip was often at a loss to pay his debts. We possess, for instance, the copy of a long bill from his bootmaker which he requests his father's steward to discharge " for the safeguard of his credit." Thus Leicester's marriage, which seriously impaired Philip's prospects, Lady Mary's want of cordiality toward her brother, and the poverty of the Sidneys, may be reckoned among the causes which postponed Penelope's betrothal. It should also here be noticed that Sir Henry Sidney entertained a grudge against the Earl of Essex. Writing to Lord Leicester, he couples Essex with his old enemy the Earl of Ormond, adding that " for that their malice, I take God to record, I could brook nothing of them both." We may therefore conclude that Philip's father was unfavourable to the match. But the chief cause remains to be mentioned. Up to this time the proposed bridegroom felt no lover's liking for the lady. Languet frequently wrote, urging him to marry, and using arguments similar to those which Shakespeare pressed on his " fair friend." Philip's answers show that, unless he was a deep dissembler, he remained heart-free. So time slipped by. Perhaps he thought that he might always pluck the rose by only asking for it. At any rate he displayed no eagerness, until one morning the news reached him that his Penelope was contracted to a man unworthy of her, Lord Rich. Then suddenly the flame of passion, which had smouldered so obscurely as to be unrecognised by his own heart, burst out into a blaze ; and what was worse, he discovered that Penelope too loved him. In the chapter devoted to Sidney's poetry I shall return to this subject. So much, however, had to be said here, in order to present a right conception of his character. For at least four years, between the death of Essex, in September 1576, and Penelope's marriage, which we may place in the spring or summer of 1581, he was aware that her father with his last breath had blessed their union. Yet he never moved a step or showed any eagerness until it was too late. It seems that this grave youth, poet as he was, passionate lover as he undoubtedly became, and hasty as he occasionally showed himself in trifles, had a somewhat politic and sluggish temperament. Fulke Greville recorded that he never was a boy ; Languet could chide him for being sad beyond his years ; he wrote himself, amid the distractions of Venetian society, that he required hard studies to drive away melancholy. Moreover, he indulged dreams of high and noble ambition. Self-culture, the preparation of his whole nature for some great task in life, occupied his thoughts to the exclusion of a woman's image. This saved him from the faults and follies of his age ; but it rendered him cold, until the poet's fire leaped up and kindled a slumbering emotion.

Not love, but the ambition of a statesman, then was
Sidney's ruling passion at this time. He had no mind
to "sport with Amaryllis in the shade," or even to
"meditate the thankless Muse," when work could be
done for England and the affairs of Europe called for
energetic action. In the spring of 1577 Elizabeth
selected him for a mission, which flattered these aspirations. Rodolph of Hapsburg had just succeeded to the
imperial throne, and the Elector Palatine had died, leaving two sons, Lewis and John Casimir. She sent Philip
to congratulate the emperor and to condole with the
bereaved princes. He stipulated that, after performing
the ceremonial part of this embassy, he should be permitted to confer with the German Powers upon the best
means of maintaining reformed principles and upholding
political liberties. Instructions were accordingly drawn
up which empowered the youthful envoy to touch upon
these points. At the end of February he set out upon
his travels, attended by Fulke Greville and by a train of
gentlefolk. In the houses where he lodged he caused
tablets to be fixed, emblazoned with his arms, under
which ran a Latin inscription to this effect : " Of the
most illustrous and well-born English gentleman, Philip
Sidney, son of the Viceroy of Ireland, nephew of the
Earls of Warwick and Leicester, Ambassador from the
most Serene Queen of England to the Emperor." This
ostentation was not out of harmony with the pompous
habits of that age. Yet we may perhaps discern in it
Sidney's incapacity to treat his own affairs with lightness.
He took himself and all that concerned him *au serieux;*
but it must also be observed that he contrived to make
others accept him in like manner. As Jonson puts it,

when comparing himself, under the name of Horace, with
men of less sterling merit :

> " If they should confidently praise their works,
>   In them it would appear inflation ;
>   Which, in a full and well-digested man,
>   Cannot receive that foul abusive name,
>   But the fair title of erection."

He first proceeded to Heidelberg, where he failed to find
the Elector Lewis, but made acquaintance with the
younger prince, his brother Casimir. The palatinate, like
many of the petty German states, was torn by religious
factions. The last elector had encouraged Calvinism ;
but his son Lewis was now introducing Lutheran ministers
into his dominions. The Calvinists, after enduring considerable hardships, had to emigrate ; and many of them
took refuge with Prince Casimir. It seems that before
he reached Heidelberg, Sidney had been met by Hubert
Languet ; and this good counsellor attended him through
all his German wanderings. They went together to
Prague, where the new emperor was holding his Court.
Here, even more than at Heidelberg, the English Envoy
found matter for serious disquietude. Rodolph had grown
up under Catholic influences, and the Jesuits were gain-
ing firm hold upon his capital. Students of history will
remember that a Jesuit Father had negotiated the participation of the Emperor Ferdinand in the closing
of the Tridentine Council. Austria, under his grandson
Rodolph's rule, bid fair to become one of their advanced
posts in northern Europe. Sidney meant, so far as in
him lay, to shake the prestige of this " extremely Spanio-
lated " and priest-ridden emperor. It was his intention
to harangue in Germany against the " fatal conjunction

of Rome's undermining superstition with the commanding forces of Spain." Fulke Greville has sketched the
main line of his argument; but it is hardly probable
that he bearded the lion in his den and spoke his mind
out before the imperial presence. The substance of the
policy he strove to impress upon those German princes
who took the Protestant side, and upon all well-wishers
to the people, was that the whole strength of their great
nation could nŏt save them from the subtle poison which
Sarpi styled the Diacatholicon, unless they made a vigor-
ous effort of resistance. Rome, by her insidious arts
and undermining engines—by her Jesuits and casuistical
sophistications—sapped the social fabric and dissolved
the ancestral loyalties of races. Into the dismembered
and disintegrated mass marched Spain with her might of
arms, her money, her treaties, marriages, and encouragement of sedition. In short, Sidney uttered a prophecy of
what happened in the Thirty Years War, that triumph of
Jesuitical diplomacy. As a remedy he proposed that
all the German Powers who valued national independence, and had a just dread of Spanish encroachment,
should "associate by an uniform bond of conscience for
the protection of religion and liberty." In other words,
he espoused the policy of what was known as the *Fœdus
Evangelicum*.

Theoretically, this plan was not only excellent, but also
necessary for stemming the advance of those reactionary
forces, knit together by bonds of common interest and
common enthusiasm, which governed the Counter Reformation. But unfortunately it rested upon no solid basis
of practical possibilities. A Protestant Alliance, formed to
secure the political and religious objects of the Reforma-

tion in its warfare with Catholicism, had been the cherished scheme of northern statesmen since the days of Henry VIII. The principles of evangelical piety, of national freedom, of progressive thought, and of Teutonic emancipation upon regulated methods, might perhaps have been established, if the Church of England could have combined with the Lutherans of Germany, the Calvinists of Geneva and of France, Sweden, and the Low Countries, in a solid confederation for the defence of civil and religious liberty. But from the outset, putting national jealousies and diplomatic difficulties aside, there existed in the very spirit of Protestantism a power antagonistic to cohesion. Protestantism had its root in critical and sceptical revolt. From the first it assumed forms of bewildering diversity on points of doctrine. Each of its sects passed at an early stage into dogmatism, hardly less stubborn than that of the Catholic Church. It afforded no common or firm ground-work for alliance. Lutherans, Zwinglians, Anglicans, Anabaptists, Hussites, Calvinists, Sacramentarians, Puritans, could not work together for a single end. It has always been thus with the party of progress, the Liberals of world-transforming moments in the march of thought. United by no sanctioned *Credo*, no fixed *Corpus Fidei*, no community of Conservative tradition; owing no allegiance to a spiritual monarch; depending for their being on rebellion against authority and discipline; disputing the fundamental propositions from which organisation has hitherto been expanded,—they cannot act in concert. These men are innovators, scene-shifters, to whom the new scene, as in the plan of God it will appear, is still invisible. They are movers from a fixed

point to a point yet unascertained. Each section into
which they crystallise, and where as sects they sterilise,
conceives the coming order according to its narrow pre-
judices. Each sails toward the haven of the future by
its own ill-balanced compass, and observes self-chosen
stars. The very instinct for change, the very apprehen-
sion which sets so-called Reformers in motion, implies
individualities of opinion and incompatibilities of will.
Therefore they are collectively weak when ranged
against the ranks of orthodoxy and established discipline.
It is only because the life of the world beats in their
hearts and brains, because the onward faces of humanity
are with them, that they command our admiration. The
victory of liberalism in modern Europe was won at the
cost of retrograde movements—such as the extinction of
free thought in Italy and Spain, the crushing of the
Huguenots in France, the bloody persecution of the
Netherlands, the Thirty Years War, and the ossification
of the Reformed Churches into inorganic stupidity. And
the fruits of the victory fall not to any sect of Protestantism, but to a new spirit which arose in Science and
the Revolution. To expect, therefore, as Sidney and the
men with whom he sympathised expected, that a Protestant League could be formed, capable of hurling back
the tide of Catholic reaction, was little short of the indulgence of a golden dream. Facts and the essence of
the Reformation were against its possibility. As a
motive force in the world, Protestantism was already
well-nigh exhausted. Its energy had already passed
into new forms. The men of the future were now
represented by philosophers like Bruno and Bacon, by
navigators of the world like Drake, by explorers of the

heavens like Galileo, by anatomists and physicists like Vesalius, Servetus, Sarpi, Harvey.

Whatever Sidney's hopes and dreams may have been, the religious discords of Germany, torn asunder by Protestant sectarians and worm-eaten to the core by Jesuitical propagandists, must have rudely disilluded him. And no one was better fitted than Languet to dissect before his eyes the humours and imposthumes of that unwieldy body politic. They left Prague at the end of April, travelled together to Heidelberg, visited the Landgrave of Hesse, and arrived at Cologne in May. Here Sidney thought that he must turn his face immediately homewards, though he greatly wished to pass into Flanders. Languet dissuaded him, on grounds of prudence, from doing so without direct commission from the queen. Great therefore was the satisfaction of both when letters arrived from England, ordering Sidney to compliment William the Silent, Prince of Orange, on the birth of his son. During this visit to the Netherlands he made acquaintance with the two most distinguished men there, and won the respect of both. Don John of Austria, the victor of Lepanto, was then acting as viceroy to the King of Spain. Sidney paid him his respects, and this is the account Fulke Greville gives of his reception :—

"Though at the first, in his Spanish haughture, he (Don John) gave him access as by descent to a youth, of grace as to a stranger, and in particular competition, as he conceived, to an enemy; yet after a while that he had taken his just altitude, he found himself so stricken with this extraordinary planet that the beholders wondered to see what ingenuous tribute that brave and high-minded prince paid to his worth, giving more honour and respect to this hopeful young gentleman than to the ambassadors of mighty princes."

What happened at Sidney's interview with William of Orange is not told us. That he made a strong impression on the stadtholder appears from words spoken to Fulke Greville after some years. Greville had been sent as ambassador to the prince at Delft. Among other things William bade him report to Queen Elizabeth his opinion "that her Majesty had one of the ripest and greatest counsellors of estate in Sir Philip Sidney that at this day lived in Europe; to the trial of which he was pleased to leave his own credit engaged until her Majesty might please to employ this gentleman either amongst her friends or enemies." Sidney's caution prevented his friend from delivering this message to a sovereign notoriously jealous of foreign interference in her home affairs.

Philip was in London again in June, when he presented his respects to her Majesty at Greenwich. That he had won credit by the discharge of his embassy appears from a letter written by Mr. Secretary Walsingham to Sir Henry Sidney soon after his arrival. "There hath not been any gentleman, I am sure, these many years that hath gone through so honourable a charge with as great commendations as he: in consideration whereof I could not but communicate this part of my joy with your Lordship, being no less a refreshing unto me in these my troublesome businesses than the soil is to the chafed stag." Henceforth we may regard our hero as a courtier high in favour with the queen, esteemed for his solid parts by the foremost statesmen of the realm, in correspondence with the leaders of the Reformed party on the Continent, and surely marked out for some employment of importance. He had long to wait, however, before that craving for action in the great world which we have already indicated as his leading passion, could even in part be gratified. Meanwhile it was his duty to hang about the Court ; and how irksome he found that petty sphere of compliments, intrigues, and gallantries, can be read in the impatient letters he addressed to Languet. Their correspondence was pretty regularly maintained, although the old man sometimes grumbled at his young friend's want of attention. " Weigh well, I beseech you, what it is to grudge through so long a space of time one single hour to friends who love you so dearly, and who are more anxious for you than for themselves. By omitting one dance a month you could have abundantly satisfied us." In this strain Languet writes occasionally. But his frequent reference to Philip's " sweetest letters," and the familiarity he always displays with his private affairs, show that the young courtier was a tolerably regular correspondent. It is difficult for elderly folk, when they have conceived ardent affection for their juniors, to remember how very much more space the young occupy in the thoughts of the old than the old can hope to command in youthful brains distracted by the multifarious traffic of society. Languet had little to do but to ply his pen in his study. Sidney had to follow the queen on progress, trifle with her ladies, join in games of skill and knightly exercises with the gentlemen about the Court. Yet it is certain that this life wearied him. He was for ever seeking to escape ; at one time planning to join Prince Casimir in the Low Countries ; at another to take part in Frobisher's expedition ; and more than once contemplating " some Indian project." Languet did his best to curb these wandering ambitions. He had conceived a very firm opinion that Sidney was born to be a statesman, not a soldier of fortune, not an explorer of the ocean. At the same time, he greatly dreaded lest his friend should succumb to the allurements of fashionable idleness. "My noble Sidney, you must avoid that persistent siren, sloth." "Think not that God endowed you with parts so excellent to the end that you should let them rot in leisure. Rather hold firmly that He requires more from you than from those to whom He has been less liberal of talents." "There is no reason to fear lest you should decay in idleness if only you will employ your mind; for in so great a realm as England opportunity will surely not be wanting for its useful exercise." "Nature has adorned you with the richest gifts of mind and body; fortune with noble blood and wealth and splendid family connections; and you from your first boyhood have cultivated your intellect by those studies which are most helpful to men in their struggle after virtue. Will you then refuse your energies to your country when it demands them? Will you bury that distinguished talent God has given you?" The career Languet had traced out for Philip was that of a public servant; and he consistently strove to check the young man's restlessness, to overcome his discouragement, and to stimulate him while depressed by the frivolities of daily life. It was his object to keep Philip from roaming or wasting his powers on adventure, while he also fortified his will against the seductions of an idle Court.

During this summer of 1577 Languet once or twice alludes in very cautious language to some project

of great importance which had recently been mooted
between them on the Continent. It involved the
participation of eminent foreigners. It required the
sanction and active assistance of the queen. What
this was we do not know. Some of Sidney's biographers are of opinion that it concerned his marriage
with a German noblewoman. Others—perhaps with
better reason—conjecture that his candidature for the
Polish Crown had then been mooted. When Henri III.
resigned the throne of Poland for that of France in 1574
Stephen Bathori was elected king. He lived until 1585.
But in 1577, the year of Languet's mysterious letters,
he had not yet given substantial proof of his future
policy ; and the Protestant party in Europe might have
been glad to secure a nominee of the English queen as
candidate in the case of a vacancy. There is no doubt
that a belief prevailed after Sidney's death that the
crown of Poland had in some sort been offered him.
The author of *The Life and Death of Sir Philip Sidney*
mentions it. Sir Robert Naunton asserts that the queen
refused " to further his advancement, not only out of
emulation, but out of fear to lose the jewel of her times."
Fuller says that Sidney declined the honour, preferring
to be " a subject to Queen Elizabeth than a sovereign
beyond the seas." It would be far too flattering to Philip
to suppose that a simple English gentleman in his twenty-
third year received any actual offer of a throne which
a king of France had recently vacated, and which was
generally given by election to such as could afford to pay
dearly for the honour. Yet it is not impossible that
the Reformed princes of Germany may have thought him
a good pawn to play, if Elizabeth were willing to back

him. The *Fœdus Evangelicum*, it must be remembered, was by no means yet devoid of actuality.

Mary Sidney's recent marriage to the Earl of Pembroke had strengthened the family by an alliance with one of England's chief noblemen. After coming home Philip paid his sister a visit at Wilton, returning, however, soon to Court in order to watch his father's interests. Sir Henry Sidney was still at his post as Lord Deputy of Ireland ; and in his absence the usual intrigues were destroying his credit with the queen. Brilliant, unscrupulous, mendacious, Ormond poured calumnies and false insinuations into her ear. She gave the earl too easy credence, partly because he was handsome, and partly because the government of Ireland was always costing money. There seems little doubt that Sir Henry made no pecuniary profit for himself out of his viceroyalty, and that he managed the realm as economically and as justly as was possible. Ormond and the nobles of his party, however, complained that the Lord Deputy decided cases inequitably against them, that his method of government was ruinously expensive, and that he tyrannously exacted from them land-taxes which had been remitted by his predecessors. Philip undertook his father's defence in a written statement, only the rough notes of which, and those imperfect, have come down to us. He met the charge of injustice by challenging the accusers to show evidence. On the question of the land-tax, or cess, which Ormond and others claimed to have remitted, he proved the inequity and the political imprudence of freeing great nobles from burdens which must be paid by the poor. These poor, moreover, were already taxed by their lords, and shamefully ill-treated by them. "And privileged persons, forsooth, be all the rich men of the pale, the burden only lying upon the poor, who may groan, for their cry cannot be heard." Sir Henry had proposed to convert the cess, computed at an average of ten pounds, into a fixed annual payment of five marks. At this the nobles cried out that they were being robbed. Philip demonstrated that, according to their own showing, a very easy compromise had been offered them. On the head of economy, he was able to make it clear that his father's administration tended to save money to the State, allowing always for the outlay needed by an army in occupation of a turbulent and disaffected country. Such a government as that of Ireland could not be conducted cheaper. But some had urged that the Lord Deputy exceeded measure in the severity of his justice and the cruelty of his executive. Philip contended that a greater lenity than that which his father showed would have been worse than folly. What he wrote upon this point is worthy of careful perusal at the present day. It reminds us that the Irish difficulty has been permanent, and without appreciable alteration, through three centuries. "Little is lenity to prevail in minds so possessed with a natural inconstancy ever to go in a new fortune, with a revengeful hate to all English as to their only conquerors, and that which is most of all, with so ignorant obstinacy in Papistry that they do in their souls detest the present Government." And again : "Truly the general nature of all countries not fully conquered is against it (*i.e.* against gentle dealing and concessions). For until by time they find the sweetness of due subjection, it is impossible that any gentle means should put out the remembrance of their

lost liberty. And that the Irishman is that way as
obstinate as any nation, with whom no other passion can
prevail but fear (besides their history, which plainly
points it out), their manner of life, wherein they choose
rather all filthiness than any law, and their own con-
sciences, who best know their own natures, give sufficient
proof of. For under the sun there is not a nation that
live more tyrannously than they do one over the other."

This defence seems to have satisfied Elizabeth and
exculpated the Lord Deputy, without impairing its
writer's credit at Court. It is the first of a series of semi-
official documents, in which, more perhaps than in any
other species of composition, Sidney showed his power
as a master of language. Waterhouse wrote to Sir
Henry that it was the most excellent discourse he had
ever read, adding, "Let no man compare with Sir Philip's
pen." During the dispute, and before the queen had
expressed her satisfaction with the Lord Deputy's defence, Ormond addressed some remarks to Philip in the
presence of the Court. The young man made no reply,
marking his hostility by silence. It was expected that
a duel would follow upon this affront to the great Irish
earl. But Ormond, judging it expedient to treat
Sidney as a virtuous gentleman who was bound to defend his father's cause, conceded him the indulgence of
a superior.

The storm which threatened Sir Henry Sidney blew
over, in great measure owing to his son's skilful advo-
cacy. Still Elizabeth retained her grudge against the
Viceroy. He had not yet contrived to flatter that most
sensitive member of the royal person—her pocket.
Consequently, the year 1578 scarcely opened before new

grievances arose. The queen talked of removing Sir Henry from his office—with, perchance, the cumbrous honour of a peerage. He, on the other hand, presented bills to the amount of three thousand and one pounds, for money disbursed from his private estate in the course of public business. She refused to sign a warrant for their payment, alleging, apparently, that the Lord Deputy was creating debts of State in his own interest. Sir Henry retorted—and all the extant documents tend to the belief that his retort was true—that he had spent thus much of his own monies upon trust for her Majesty; and that he needed the sum, barring one pound, for the payment of his daughter's marriage portion to the Earl of Pembroke. Perusal of the correspondence seems to me to prove that, however bad a diplomatist and stubborn a viceroy Sir Henry may have been, he was, at any rate, a thoroughly honest man. And this honest man's debts, contracted in her name and in her service, the queen chose to repudiate. It is not wonderful that, under these circumstances, the Lord Deputy thought of throwing up his appointment and retiring into private life in England. Philip's persuasions induced his father to abandon this design. He pointed out that the term of office would expire at Michaelmas, and that it would be more for the Deputy's credit to tender his resignation at that time without an open rupture. One of his letters shows how valuable in these domestic counsels was the Lady Mary Sidney. Philip writes that in the meantime—that is, between Ladyday and Michaelmas—Sir Henry's friends would do their best to heal the breach; "Among which friends, before God, there is none proceeds either so thoroughly or so

wisely as your lady, my mother.   For mine own part, I
have had only light from her."

These sentences afford a very pleasing insight into
the relations between father, mother, and eldest son.
But the tension of the situation for Philip at Court,
playing his part as queen's favourite while his father
was disgraced, shouldering the Irish braggarts whom
she protected, and who had declared war against her
viceroy, presenting a brave front before the world, with
only an impoverished estate to back him,—the tension
of this situation must have been too great for his
sensitive nerves.   We find that he indulged suspicions.
Things transpired at Court which he believed had been
committed only in most private correspondence to Sir
Henry.   He wrote to his father : "I must needs impute
it to some men about you that there is little written
from you or to you that is not perfectly known to your
professed enemies."   A few weeks after penning these
words he thought that he had caught the culprit in Mr.
Edmund Molineux, Sir Henry's secretary.   This explains
the following furious epistle, which no biographer of
Sidney should omit in its proper place :—

"MR. MOLINEUX—Few words are best.   My letters to
my father have come to the ears of some : neither can I condemn any but you.   If it be so, you have played the very
knave with me ; and so I will make you know, if I have
good proof of it.   But that for so much as is past.   For that
is to come, I assure you, before God, that if ever I know you
to do so much as read any letter I write to my father without
his commandment or my consent, I will thrust my dagger
into you.   And trust to it, for I speak in earnest.   In the
meantime, farewell.—From Court, this last of May 1578.
By me,   PHILIP SIDNEY."

Philip had made a great mistake—a mistake not unlike that which betrayed him into false judgment of his comrade Coningsby. Molineux was as true as steel to his father, as loyal as Abdiel to the house of Sidney. It was he who composed for Hollingshed the heartfelt panegyrics of Sir Henry, Sir Philip, and Lady Mary. On this occasion he met the young man's brutal insults with words which may have taught him courtesy. The letter deserves to be given in its integrity :—

" Sir—I have received a letter from you which as it is the first so the same is the sharpest that I ever received from any ; and therefore it amazeth me the more to receive such an one from you, since I have (the world can judge) deserved better somewhere, howsoever it pleased you to condemn me now. But since it is (I protest to God) without cause, or yet just ground of suspicion, you use me thus, I bear the injury more patiently for a time, and mine innocency I hope in the end shall try mine honesty, and then I trust you will confess that you have done me wrong. And since your pleasure so is expressed that I shall not henceforth read any of your letters (although I must confess I have heretofore taken both great delight and profit in reading some of them) yet upon so hard a condition as you seem to offer, I will not hereafter adventure so great peril, but obey you herein. Howbeit, if it had pleased you, you might have commanded me in a far greater matter with a less penalty.—Yours, when it shall please you better to conceive of me, humbly to command,   F. Molineux."

We doubt not that Philip made honourable amends for his unjust imputations, since good friendship afterwards subsisted between him and Molineux. The incident, on which I have thought fit to dwell, reveals something not altogether pleasing in our hero's character. But the real deduction to be drawn from

it is that his position at this time was well-nigh intolerable.

In the midst of these worrying cares he remained in
attendance on the queen. It seems that he journeyed
with the Court in all her progresses; and in May he
formed part of the royal company which Leicester
welcomed to his house at Wanstead. The entertainment
provided for her Majesty was far simpler than that so
famous one at Kenilworth in 1575. Yet it has for us a
special interest, inasmuch as here Philip produced his
first literary essay. This was a rural masque entitled,
The Lady of the May. How it came to be written we
know not; peradventure at two sittings, between the
evening's dance and retirement to bed. The thing is
slight and without salt. If it were not still quoted in
the list of Sidney's works, we should not notice it; and
why it ever was printed I am unable to conjecture,
except upon the supposition that even in Elizabeth's
days the last drops from a famous pen, however dull
they were, found publishers. Of dramatic conception or
of power in dialogue it shows nothing; nor are the
lyrics tuneful. There is plenty of flattery introduced,
apparently to glut the queen's appetite for mud-honey,
but yet so clumsily applied as to suggest a suspicion
whether the poet were not laughing at her. The only
character which reveals force of portraiture and humour
is that of Rombus, the pedagogue, into whose mouth
Sidney has put some long-winded speeches, satirising
the pedantic and grossly ignorant style in vogue among
village schoolmasters. Rombus, in fact, is a very rough
sketch for the picture of Master Holofernes; as may be
judged by his exordium to Queen Elizabeth—

" *Stage Direction.*—Then came forward Master Rombus,
    and, with many special graces, made this learned
    oration :—

" Now the thunder-thumping Jove transfund his dotes
into your excellent formosity, which have, with your re-
splendent beams, thus segregated the enmity of these rural
animals : I am ' potentissima domina,' a school-master ; that
is to say, a pedagogue, one not a little versed in the discip-
linating of the juvenile fry, wherein, to my laud I say it, I
use such geometrical proportion, as neither wanted mansue-
tude nor correction : for so it is described—

" ' Parcare subjectos, et debellire superbos.'

Yet hath not the pulchritude of my virtues protected me
from the contaminating hands of these plebeians ; for coming,
' solummodo,' to have parted their sanguinolent fray, they
yielded me no more reverence than if I had been some
' pecorius asinus.' I, even I, that am, who am I ? 'Dixi ;
verbus sapiento satum est.' But what said that Trojan Æneas,
when he sojourned in the surging sulks of the sandiferous
seas ?

" ' Haec olim memonasse juvebit.'

Well, well, ' ad propositos revertebo ;' the purity of the
verity is, that a certain ' pulchra puella profecto,' elected
and constituted by the integrated determination of all this
topographical region, as the sovereign lady of this dame
Maia's month, hath been, 'quodammodo,' hunted, as you
would say ; pursued by two, a brace, a couple, a cast of
young men, to whom the crafty coward Cupid had, ' inquam,'
delivered his dire dolorous dart."

During this summer Philip obtained a place at Court,
the importance of which his friend Languet seems to
have exaggerated. Zouch says it was the post of cup-
bearer to the queen ; and in this statement there is no
improbability, but there is also nothing to warrant it.
At any rate the office failed to satisfy his ambition ; for

he wrote complainingly, as usual, of the irksomeness of
Court existence. How disagreeable that must in some
respects have been is made clear to us by Lady Mary's
letters in the autumn of this year. She was expecting
her husband home from Ireland. He had to reside
with her at Hampton Court, where she could only call
one bedroom her own. To the faithful Molineux she
writes :—

"I have thought good to put you in remembrance to
move my Lord Chamberlain in my Lord's name, to have
some other room than my chamber for my Lord to have his
resort unto, as he was wont to have ; or else my Lord will
be greatly troubled, when he shall have any matters of
despatch : my lodgings, you see, being very little, and myself
continually sick and not able to be much out of my bed.
For the night-time one roof, with God's grace, shall serve
us. For the daytime, the queen will look to have my
chamber always in a readiness for her Majesty's coming
thither ; and though my Lord himself can be no impediment
thereto by his own presence, yet his Lordship, trusting to
no place else to be provided for him, will be, as I said
before, troubled for want of a convenient place for the despatch of such people as shall have occasion to come to him.
Therefore, I pray you, in my Lord's own name, move my
Lord of Sussex for a room for that purpose, and I will have
it hanged and lined for him with stuff from hence. I wish
you not to be unmindful hereof ; and so for this time I
leave you to the Almighty.—From Chiswick this 11th
October 1578."

It would appear that Lady Mary's very modest
request for a second room, which she undertook to
furnish out of her own wardrobe, was not at once
granted. Another letter to Molineux shows that he
had made some progress in the matter, but had not
succeeded. Hampton Court, she writes, however full it

may be, has always several spare rooms.   Perhaps there
are those who "will be sorry my Lord should have
so sure footing in the Court."   Could not Molineux
contrive the loan of a parlour for her husband in the
daytime ?   Yet, after all, "when the worst is known,
old Lord Harry and his old Moll will do as well as they
can in parting, like good friends, the small portion
allotted our long service in Court."   There is something
half pathetic and half comic in the picture thus presented
to our minds of the great Duke of Northumberland's
daughter, with her husband, the Viceroy of Ireland and
Wales, dwelling at hugger-mugger in one miserable
chamber—she well-nigh bedridden, he transacting his
business in a corner of it, and the queen momently
expected upon visitations, not always, we may guess, of
friendship or affection.   Yet the touch of homely humour
in the last sentence I have quoted from the noble lady's
letter, sheds a pleasant light upon the sordid scene.

Studying the details of Court life both in Italy and
England at this period, we are often led to wonder why
noblemen with spacious palaces and venerable mansions of
their own to dwell in—why men of genius whose brilliant
gifts made them acceptable in every cultivated circle—
should have submitted so complacently to its ignoble conditions.   Even those who seemed unable to breathe outside the sphere of the Court spoke most bitterly against it.
Tasso squandered his health, his talents, nay, his reason,
in that servitude.   Guarini, after impairing his fortune,
and wasting the best years of his manhood at Ferrara,
retired to a country villa, and indulged his spleen in
venomous invectives against the vices and the ignominies
he had abandoned.   Marino, who flaunted his gay

plumage at Turin and Paris, screamed like a cockatoo with cynical spite whenever the word Court was mentioned. The only wise man of that age in Italy was the literary bravo Aretino. He, having debauched his youth in the vilest places of the Roman Courts, resolved to live a free man henceforth. Therefore he took refuge in Venice, where he caressed his sensual appetites and levied blackmail on society. From that retreat, which soon became a sty of luxury, he hurled back upon the Courts the filth which he had gathered in them. His dialogue on Court service is one of the most savage and brutally naked exposures of depravity which satirical literature contains. In England there was indeed a far higher tone of manliness and purity and personal independence at the Court than obtained in Italy. Yet listen to Spenser's memorable lines, obviously poured forth from the heart and coloured by bitterest experience :—

> "Full little knowest thou, that hast not tried,
>   What hell it is in suing long to bide :
>   To lose good days, that might be better spent ;
>   To waste long nights in pensive discontent ;
>   To speed to-day, to be put back to-morrow ;
>   To feed on hope, to pine with fear and sorrow ;
>   To have thy prince's grace, yet want her peers' ;
>   To have thy asking, yet wait many years ;
>   To fret thy soul with crosses and with cares ;
>   To eat thy heart through comfortless despairs ;
>   To fawn, to crouch, to wait, to ride, to run,
>   To spend, to give, to want, to be undone :
>   Unhappy wight, born to disastrous end,
>   That doth his life in so long tendance spend !"

Therefore we return to wondering what it was in Courts which made gentlefolk convert broad acres into

cash that they might shine there, which lured noblemen
from their castles and oak-shaded deer-parks to occupy
a stuffy bedroom in a royal palace, and squires from
their moss-grown manor-houses to jolt along the roads
on horseback in attendance on a termagant like Elizabeth or a learned pig like James I. The real answer
to these questionings is that, in the transition from
mediæval to modern conditions of life, the Court had
become a social necessity for folk of a certain quality
and certain aspirations. It was the only avenue to
public employment; the only sphere in which a man of
ambition, who was neither clerk in orders nor lawyer,
could make his mark; the only common meeting-
ground for rank, beauty, wealth, and genius. Thus it
exercised a splendid fascination, the reflex of which is
luminous in our dramatic literature. After reading
those sad and bitter lines of Spenser, we should turn
to the pages of Fletcher's *Valentinian*, where the allurements of the Court are eloquently portrayed in the great
scene of Lucina's attempted seduction. Or better, let
us quote the ecstasies of Fortunatus from the most
fanciful of Dekker's plays :—

" For still in all the regions I have seen,
    I scorned to crowd among the muddy throng
    Of the rank multitude, whose thickened breath,
    Like to condensed fogs, do choke that beauty
    Which else would dwell in every kingdom's cheek.
    No, I still boldly stepped into their courts,
    For there to live 'tis rare, oh, 'tis divine !
    There shall you see faces angelical ;
    There shall you see troops of chaste goddesses,
    Whose star-like eyes have power (might they still shine)
    To make night day, and day more crystalline :
    Near these you shall behold great heroës,

> White-headed counsellors, and jovial spirits,
> Standing like fiery cherubims to guard
> The monarch who in god-like glory sits
> In midst of these, as if this deity
> Had with a look created a new world,
> The standers-by being the fair workmanship."

Philip, like so many of his contemporaries, continued to waver between the irresistible attraction of the Court and the centrifugal force which urged him to be up and doing, anywhere, at any occupation, away from its baneful and degrading idleness. Just now, in the summer of 1578, he was hankering to join his friend, John Casimir, at Zutphen. Elizabeth had nominated this prince to her lieutenancy in the Low Countries, supplying him with money in small quantities for the levying of troops. When he took the field, Philip burned to accept an invitation sent him by the prince. But first he had to gain his father's permission. Sir Henry's answer is the model of kindness and of gentle unselfishness. He begins by acknowledging the honour paid his son, and commending Philip's eagerness. But "when I enter into the consideration of mine own estate, and call to mind what practices, informations, and wicked accusations are devised against me, and what an assistance in the defence of those causes your presence would be unto me, reposing myself so much both upon your help and judgment, I strive betwixt honour and necessity what allowance I may best give of that motion for your going." Then he goes on to say that he leaves the consideration of these matters to his son, and will in no way check his inclination or refuse his consent. Philip sacrificed his wishes, and

remained in England to assist his father. This act of
filial compliance cost him, as it happened, nothing; for
Casimir's dealings in the Netherlands brought no credit
to himself or his companions. None the less should
we appreciate the amiable trait in Sidney's character.

Sir Henry returned in due course to England in the
autumn, and tendered his resignation of the Irish Viceroyalty. He still maintained his post as Lord President
of Wales. On New Year's Day, 1579, presents were
exchanged, as usual, between Elizabeth and her chief
courtiers. Poor Sir Henry, out of pocket as he was,
presented her Majesty with a jewel of gold, diamonds,
pearls, and rubies, upon which was wrought a figure of
Diana. She returned a hundred and thirty-eight ounces
of gold plate. Lady Mary and Philip offered articles of
dress, receiving their equivalent in plate. Prince Casimir,
who had to answer for his malconduct of affairs in
the Low Countries, reached London in the month of
January. The queen gave him a gracious reception.
He was nominated to a stall in St. George's chapel, and
entertained with various amusements. Among other
sports, we hear that he shot a stag in Hyde Park. On
the 12th of February he again left England with presents
from the queen. A letter of the day significantly
alludes to her unwilling bestowal of money on the
prince: "'There hath been somewhat to do to bring her
unto it, and Mr. Secretary Walsingham bare the brunt
thereof."

One incident of Casimir's visit must not be omitted.
Hubert Languet, old as he now was, and failing in health,
resolved to set his eyes once more on his beloved Philip.
"I am almost afraid," he wrote in January, "that my

great desire of seeing you may betray me into thinking
I am better than I am, yet I will do my very utmost to
be ready for the journey, even though I should take it
at the peril of my life." He came and went safely, had
the pleasure of conversing with Philip, and made friends
with the chief members of the Sidney family. A letter
written in the autumn of the next year shows that this
experienced judge of men and cities formed no very
favourable opinion of the English Court. "I was pleased
last winter to find you flourishing in favour, and highly
esteemed by all men. Yet, to conceal nothing, it
appeared to me that the manners of your Court are less
manly than I could wish; and the majority of your great
folk struck me as more eager to gain applause by affected
courtesy, than by such virtues as benefit the commonwealth, and are the chief ornament of noble minds and
high-born personages. It grieved me then, as also your
other friends, that you should waste the flower of your
youth in such trifles. I began to fear lest your excellent
disposition should at last be blunted, lest you should
come by habit to care for things which soften and emas-
culate our mind."

We have already seen that Sidney was not otherwise
than himself alive to these dangers, and that he chafed
continually at the "expense of spirit in a waste" of
frivolities. As a couplet in one of his occasional poems
puts it—

> "Greater was the shepherd's treasure,
> Than this false, fine, courtly pleasure."

From the same poem we learn that his friendship for
Fulke Greville and Edward Dyer continued to be his

mainstay at the Court; and when I enter upon the details of his literary career, it will become apparent that much of his time had been already spent with these and other cultivated gentlefolk in the prosecution of serious studies. For the present it seems better not to interrupt the history of his external life.

CHAPTER IV

THE FRENCH MATCH AND "THE ARCADIA"

THE years 1579 and 1580 are of importance in the biography of Sidney, owing to the decided part he took in the discussion of the French match. Elizabeth's former suitor, d'Alençon, now bore the title of Duke of Anjou, by his brother Henri's accession to the throne of France. Time had cast a decent veil over the memory of St. Bartholomew, and Anjou was now posing as the protector of national liberties in the Low Countries. He thought the opportunity good for renewing negotiations with the Queen of England. That the Court of the Valois was anxious to arrange the marriage admits of no doubt. The sums of money spent in presents and embassies render this certain, for Catherine de' Medici and her sons were always in pecuniary difficulties. They could not afford to throw gold away on trifles.

Elizabeth showed a strong inclination to accept the duke's proposal. She treated his envoy, Du Simiers, with favour, and kept up a brisk correspondence with Paris. The match, however, was extremely unpopular with the English people. In the autumn of 1579 there appeared a pamphlet entitled: "The Discovery of the Gaping Gulf, whereinto England is like to be swal-

lowed, by a French marriage, if the Lord forbid not the
Banns, by letting her Majesty see the Sin and Punishment thereof." This sufficed to indicate the temper of
the best part of the nation, the Protestants, who saw
their religious and political liberties in danger. Stubbs
and Page, the author and the printer of this " lewd and
seditious book," as it was termed by royal proclamation,
were each condemned to lose the right hand. Stubbs,
when the hangman had performed his office, waved his
hat with the left hand, crying " God save the Queen ! "
Page pointed to his bloody hand upon the ground, and
said, " There lies the hand of a true Englishman ! "

At Court opinion was divided. Elizabeth's flatterers,
with Oxford at their head, declared themselves loudly
in favour of the match. Leicester opposed it ; but Du
Simiers' opportune discovery of the secret marriage with
Lady Essex ruined his credit. The great earl had to
retire in disgrace. Camden relates that the queen
banished him until further notice to Greenwich Castle.
Fulke Greville says "the French faction reigning had cast
aspersions upon his (Sidney's) uncle of Leicester, and
made him, like a wise man (under colour of taking physic)
voluntarily become prisoner in his chamber." Whether
his retirement was compulsory or voluntary matters little.
For the time he lost his influence, and was unable to
show his face at Court. Thus Philip who had already
elected to "join with the weaker party and oppose this
torrent," found himself at the moment of his greatest
need deprived of the main support which powerful connections gave him.

Greville has devoted a chapter to his action in this
matter, analysing with much detail the reasons which

F

moved him to oppose the queen's inclination. It is not
necessary to report his friend's view of the case, since I
shall shortly have to present an abstract of the famous
document which Sidney drew up for Elizabeth's perusal.
Yet the exordium to this chapter may be quoted, as
representing in brief his position at the close of 1579.

" The next doubtful stage he had to act upon (howsoever
it may seem private) was grounded upon a public and specious
proposition of marriage between the late famous queen and
the Duke of Anjou. With which current, although he saw
the great and wise men of the time suddenly carried down,
and every one fishing to catch the queen's humour in it;
yet when he considered the difference of years, person, education, state, and religion between them ; and then called to
mind the success of our former alliances with the French ; he
found many reasons to make question whether it would prove
poetical or real on their part. And if real, whether the
balance swayed not unequally, by adding much to them and
little to his sovereign. The duke's greatness being only
name and possibility ; and both these either to wither or to
be maintained at her cost. Her state, again, in hand ; and
though royally sufficient to satisfy that queen's princely and
moderate desires or expenses, yet perchance inferior to bear
out those mixed designs into which his ambition or necessities
might entice or draw her."

It came to pass, through Leicester's disgrace, that
Philip stood almost alone at Court as the resolute
opponent of the French faction. The profligate and unscrupulous Earl of Oxford, now foremost in the queen's
favour, was carrying his head aloft, boastful of his compliance with her wishes, and counting doubtless on the
highest honours when the match should be completed.
An accident brought the two champions of the opposed
parties into personal collision. One of Languet's letters

enables us to fix the date of the event in September 1579, and Greville's minute account of the same is so curious that I shall transcribe it without further comment.

"Thus stood the Court at that time ; and thus stood this ingenuous spirit in it. If dangerously in men's opinions who are curious of the present, and in it rather to do craftily than well : yet, I say, that princely heart of hers was a sanctuary unto him ; and as for the people, in whom many times the lasting images of worth are preferred before the temporary visions of art or favour, he could not fear to suffer any thing there, which would not prove a kind of trophy to him. . . . In this freedom of heart, being one day at tennis, a peer of this realm, born great, greater by alliance, and superlative in the prince's favour, abruptly came into the tennis-court ; and, speaking out of these three paramount authorities, he forgot to entreat that which he could not legally command. When, by the encounter of a steady object, finding unrespectiveness in himself (though a great lord) not respected by this princely spirit, he grew to expostulate more roughly. The returns of which style coming still from an understanding heart, that knew what was due to itself and what it ought to others, seemed (through the mists of my lord's passion, swollen with the wind of this faction then reigning) to provoke in yielding. Whereby, the less amazement or confusion of thoughts he stirred up in Sir Philip, the more shadows this great lord's own mind was possessed with ; till at last with rage (which is ever ill-disciplined) he commands them to depart the court. To this Sir Philip temperately answers ; that if his lordship had been pleased to express desire in milder characters, perchance he might have led out those that he should now find would not be driven out with any scourge of fury. This answer (like a bellows) blowing up the sparks of excess already kindled, made my lord scornfully call Sir Philip by the name of *puppy*. In which progress of heat, as the tempest grew more and more vehement within, so did their hearts breathe out their perturbations in a more loud and shrill accent. The

French Commissioners unfortunately had that day audience in those private galleries whose windows looked into the tennis-court. They instantly drew all to this tumult : every sort of quarrels sorting well with their humours, especially this. Which Sir Philip perceiving, and rising with an inward strength by the prospect of a mighty faction against him, asked my lord with a loud voice that which he heard clearly enough before. Who (like an echo that still multiplies by reflexions) repeated this epithet of *puppy* the second time. Sir Philip, resolving in one answer to conclude both the attentive hearers and passionate actor, gave my lord a lie, impossible (as he averred) to be retorted ; in respect all the world knows, puppies are gotten by dogs and children by men.

Hereupon these glorious inequalities of fortune in his lordship were put to a kind of pause by a precious inequality of nature in this gentleman ; so that they both stood silent a while, like a dumb show in a tragedy ; till Sir Philip, sensible of his own wrong, the foreign and factious spirits that attended, and yet even in this question between him and his superior tender of his country's honour, with some words of sharp accent led the way abruptly out of the tennis-court; as if so unexpected an incident were not fit to be decided in that place. Whereof the great lord making another sense, continues his play, without any advantage of reputation, as by the standard of humours in those times it was conceived."

Thus the Earl of Oxford called Sidney a puppy ; and Sidney gave him the lie. It was judged inevitable that the former would send a challenge and a duel would ensue. But Oxford delayed to vindicate his honour. The Lords of the Council intervened, and persuaded the queen to effect a reconciliation. She pointed out to Sidney that he owed deference to a peer of the realm. "He besought her Majesty to consider that although he were a great lord by birth, alliance, and grace ; yet he was no lord over him." As free men and gentlemen the

earl and himself were equals, except in the matter of
precedency. Moreover, he reminded Elizabeth that it
had been her father's policy to shield the gentry from
the oppression of the grandees, in the wise opinion that
the Crown would gain by using the former as a balance
to the power and ambition of the latter. But having
stated his case, he seems to have deferred to her wishes.
We do not hear that apologies were made on either side.
The matter, however, dropped ; Oxford so far retaining
his resentment that Sidney's friends believed he entertained a scheme for his assassination.

After reading this passage, we may remember with
what spirit on a former occasion Philip gave the cut
direct to Ormond. It is also interesting to compare his
carriage upon both occasions with that of his nephew,
the Viscount l'Isle, who bearded James' favourite, James
Hay, at that time Viscount Doncaster, in his own
chamber. A detailed account of this incident, written
by Lord l'Isle in vindication of his honour, is printed
among the Sidney papers. It casts valuable light upon
the manners of the English Court, and illustrates the
sturdy temper of the Sidney breed.

Philip contrived apparently to keep the queen's good-
will until the beginning of 1580 ; for she accepted his
present of a crystal cup on New Year's Day. But his
position at Court was difficult. Oxford, it was commonly
believed, had planned his murder ; and being an Italianated Englishman—in other words, a devil incarnate—he
may well have entertained some project of the sort.
As the avowed champion of the opposition, wielding a
pen with which no man could compete, Sidney thought the
time had now come to bring matters to an issue by plain

utterance. Therefore he drew up a carefully-prepared
memorial, setting forth in firm but most respectful language
those arguments which seemed to him decisive against
the French match. This he presented to Elizabeth early
in 1580. Immediately after its perusal, she began to
show her resentment, and Philip, like his uncle, found it
convenient to leave the Court. His retreat was Wilton,
where he remained in privacy for seven months.

I have elsewhere remarked that Sidney showed his
powers as a thinker and prose-writer nowhere more
eminently than in documents, presenting a wide survey
of facts, marshalling a series of arguments, combining
the prudence of a statesman and the cunning of an
orator. This memorial to the queen is a gem in its own
species of composition. It well deserves the high praise
which has been given it as " at once the most eloquent
and the most courageous piece of that nature which the
age can boast. Every important view of the subject is
comprised in this letter, which is long, but at the same
time so condensed in style and so skilfully compacted
as to matter that it well deserves to be read entire ; and
must lose materially either by abridgement or omission."
In it Sidney appeals to what Fulke Greville quaintly
calls " that princely heart of hers which was a sanctuary
unto him." He enters the sanctuary with reverence, and
stands alone there, pleading like a servant before his
mistress. He speaks to Elizabeth in the character of a
simple gentleman and loyal subject, relying on no support of party, nor representing himself as the mouthpiece
of an indignant nation. This independent attitude
gives singular lucidity and beauty to his appeal. It is
the grave but modest warning of a faithful squire to

his liege lady in the hour of danger. Although extracts can do but scanty justice to the merits of Sidney's oratory, I must present such specimens as may serve as samples of his English style and display his method of exposition. He begins as follows :—

"MOST FEARED AND BELOVED, MOST SWEET AND GRACIOUS SOVEREIGN—To seek out excuses of this my boldness, and to arm the acknowledging of a fault with reasons for it, might better show I knew I did amiss, than any way diminish the attempt, especially in your judgment ; who being able to discern lively into the nature of the thing done, it were folly to hope, by laying on better colours, to make it more acceptable. Therefore, carrying no other olive branch of intercession, than the laying of myself at your feet ; nor no other insinuation, either for attention or pardon, but the true vowed sacrifice of unfeigned love ; I will, in simple and direct terms (as hoping they shall only come to your merciful eyes), set down the overflowing of my mind in this most important matter, importing, as I think, the continuance of your safety ; and as I know, the joys of my life. And because my words (I confess shallow, but coming from the deep well-spring of most loyal affection) have delivered to your most gracious ear, what is the general sum of my travelling thoughts therein ; I will now but only declare, what be the reasons that make me think, that the marriage with Monsieur will be unprofitable unto you ; then will I answer the objection of those fears, which might procure so violent a refuge."

Having finished these personal explanations, he proceeds to show that the French marriage must be considered from a double point of view, first as regarding the queen's estate, and secondly as touching her person. Her real power as "an absolute born, and accordingly respected princess," rests upon the affection of her subjects, who are now divided between Protestants and Catholics. The former,

" As their souls live by your happy government, so are they
your chief, if not your sole, strength : these, howsoever the
necessity of human life makes them lack, yet can they not
look for better conditions than presently they enjoy : these,
how their hearts will be galled, if not aliened, when they
shall see you take a husband, a Frenchman and a Papist, in
whom (howsoever fine wits may find farther dealings or
painted excuses) the very common people well know this, that
he is the son of a Jezebel of our age : that his brother made
oblation of his own sister's marriage, the easier to make
massacres of our brethren in belief : that he himself, contrary
to his promise, and all gratefulness, having his liberty and
principal estate by the Hugonot's means, did sack La Charité,
and utterly spoil them with fire and sword.   This, I say,
even at first sight, gives occasion to all, truly religious, to
abhor such a master, and consequently to diminish much of
the hopeful love they have long held to you."

The Catholics are discontented and disaffected. They
will grasp easily at any chance of a revolution in religion
and the State ; and to such folk the French match is
doubtless acceptable, not as producing good to the
commonwealth, but as offering them the opportunity of
change.

" If then the affectionate side have their affections weak-
ened, and the discontented have a gap to utter their discon-
tent, I think it will seem an ill preparative for the patient
(I mean your estate) to a great sickness."

From these general reflections upon the state of parties
in England, Sidney passes to a consideration of the Duke
of Anjou's personal qualities. The following paragraph
is marked by skilful blending of candour with reserve.
Elizabeth had declared a special partiality for the French
prince. It is her subject's duty to paint him as incon-
stant, restless in ambition, uncertain in his affections,

swayed by light-brained and factious counsellors, greedy
of power at any cost. His profession of the Catholic
faith renders him a dangerous tool in the hands of disaffected English Papists. His position as next heir to
the French Crown makes him an inconvenient consort
for the queen of Great Britain. It is not likely that a
man of his temper and pretensions should put up with a
subordinate place in his wife's kingdom. And why, asks
Sidney, has Elizabeth set her heart upon a marriage so
fraught with dangers? "Often have I heard you with
protestation say no private pleasure nor self-affection
could lead you to it." Is it because she looks forward
to the bliss of children? If so she may marry where
the disadvantages are less. But she has herself alleged
that she is moved by "fear of standing alone in respect
to foreign dealings," and also by "doubt of contempt in
them from whom you should have respect." These two
points, since they bias the queen's mind, have to be
separately entertained. Leagues are usually cemented
by the desires or the fears of the contracting parties.
What public desires have Elizabeth and the duke in
common?

"He of the Romish religion ; and if he be a man, must
needs have that man-like property to desire that all men be
of his mind : you the erector and defender of the contrary,
and the only sun that dazzleth their eyes : he French, and
desiring to make France great ; your Majesty English, and
desiring nothing less than that France should not grow great :
he, both by his own fancy and his youthful governors, embrac-
ing all ambitious hopes ; having Alexander's image in his head,
but perhaps evil-painted : your Majesty with excellent virtue
taught what you should hope, and by no less wisdom what
you may hope ; with a council renowned over all Christen-

dom for their well-tempered minds, having set the utmost of
their ambition in your favour, and the study of their souls in
your safety."

The interests and the dangers of France and England
are so diverse that these realms have no fears in common
to unite them. Elizabeth, therefore, can expect nothing
but perplexity in her foreign dealings from the match.
Is it reasonable that she should hope to secure the affection of her subjects, and to guard herself against their
contempt, by marriage with a Frenchman? Can she be
ignorant that she is the idol of her people? It is indeed
true that the succession is uncertain through lack of
heirs of her body :

"But in so lineal a monarchy, wherever the infants
suck the love of their rightful prince, who would leave the
beams of so fair a sun for the dreadful expectation of a divided
company of stars? Virtue and justice are the only bonds of
people's love ; and as for that point, many princes have lost
their crowns whose own children were manifest successors ;
and some that had their own children used as instruments of
their ruin ; not that I deny the bliss of children, but only
to show religion and equity to be of themselves sufficient
stays."

It may be demurred that scurrilous libels have been
vented against her Majesty, proving some insubordina-
tion in her subjects. She ought, however, to "care
little for the barking of a few curs." Honest Englishmen regard such attacks upon her dignity as blas-
phemous.

"No, no, most excellent lady, do not raze out the impression you have made in such a multitude of hearts ; and
let not the scum of such vile minds bear any witness against
your subjects' devotions. The only means of avoiding con-

tempt are love and fear ; love, as you have by divers means
sent into the depth of their souls, so if anything can stain
so true a form, it must be the trimming yourself not in your
own likeness, but in new colours unto them."

In other words, Sidney means that the Queen's proposed course will alienate instead of confirming the affections of the nation. He then passes to his peroration,
which I shall quote in full as a fair specimen of his
eloquence :—

"Since then it is dangerous for your state, as well because
by inward weakness (principally caused by division) it is fit
to receive harm ; since to your person it can be no way com-
fortable, you not desiring marriage ; and neither to person
nor estate he is to bring any more good than anybody ; but
more evil he may, since the causes that should drive you to
this are either fears of that which cannot happen, or by this
means cannot be prevented ; I do with most humble heart
say unto your Majesty (having assayed this dangerous help)
for your standing alone, you must take it for a singular
honour God hath done you, to be indeed the only protector
of his Church ; and yet in worldly respects your kingdom
very sufficient so to do, if you make that religion upon which
you stand, to carry the only strength, and have abroad those
that still maintain the same course ; who as long as they may
be kept from utter falling, your Majesty is sure enough from
your mightiest enemies.   As for this man, as long as he is
but Monsieur in might, and a Papist in profession, he neither
can nor will greatly shield you ; and if he get once to be
king, his defence will be like Ajax's shield, which rather
weighed them down than defended those that bare it.
Against contempt, if there be any, which I will never believe,
let your excellent virtues of piety, justice, and liberality
daily, if it be possible, more and more shine.   Let such particular actions be found out (which be easy as I think to be
done) by which you may gratify all the hearts of your people.
Let those in whom you find trust, and to whom you have
committed trust in your weighty affairs be held up in the

eyes of your subjects. Lastly, doing as you do, you shall be, as you be, the example of princes, the ornament of this age, and the most excellent fruit of your progenitors, and the perfect mirror of your posterity.—Your Majesty's faithful, humble, and obedient subject, P. SYDNEY."

In the early spring of 1580 Sidney went to stay at Wilton, and remained there during the summer. His sister, the Countess of Pembroke, for whom Jonson wrote the famous epitaph, and whom Spenser described as

> " The gentlest shepherdess that lives this day,
>   And most resembling both in shape and spright
>   Her brother dear,"

was united to him by the tenderest bonds of affection and by common literary interests. Good judges, among whom Jonson may be reckoned, valued her poetry at least as high as Philip's ; and this opinion is confirmed by what remains to us of her compositions. The accent of deep and passionate feeling which gives force to some of the *Astrophel and Stella* sonnets, is indeed lacking to her verse. But if we are right in believing that only the first forty-two psalms in their joint translation belong to him, her part in that work exhibits the greater measure of felicity. It was apparently upon this visit to Wilton that the brother and sister began to render the Psalms of David into various lyrical metres. After the Vulgate and the Prayer-Book all translations of the Psalms, even those done by Milton, seem tame and awkward. Nor can I except the Sidneys from this criticism. In an essay, then, which must of necessity be economical of space, I shall omit further notice of this version. The opportunity, however, is now given for digressing from

Philip's biography to the consideration of his place and achievements in English literature.

It is of importance to bear steadily in mind the date of Sidney's birth in order to judge correctly of his relation to predecessors and successors. Wyat, Surrey, Sackville, and Norton had already acclimatised Italian forms of poetry and classical principles of metre upon English soil. But very little of first-rate excellence can be referred to this period of our Renaissance. A form of the sonnet peculiar to English literature, and blank verse, destined to become its epic and dramatic metre, were the two chief results of these earliest innovating experiments. Fulke Greville, himself no mean poet, was born in 1554, the same year as Sidney; Raleigh had been born in 1552; Spenser and Lyly in 1553; Drayton followed in 1563; Shakespeare and Marlowe in 1564; Donne not till 1573, and Jonson one year later yet; Wyat and Surrey were both dead some while before Sidney saw the light; and Sackville, though he still lived, was not much occupied with literature. It will therefore be seen that he belonged to that intermediate group of writers, of whom Spenser was the greatest, and who preceded the brilliant burst of genius in the last decade of the sixteenth century. It was as the morning star of an unexampled day of lyric and dramatic splendour that his contemporaries hailed him.

In the year 1578 Philip attended Queen Elizabeth on one of her progresses when she stayed at Audley End, and there received the homage of some Cambridge scholars. Among these came Gabriel Harvey, a man of character and parts, but of no distinguished literary talent. He was what we now should call a doctrinaire;

yet he possessed so tough a personality as to exercise
considerable influence over his contemporaries. Harvey
enthusiastically declared himself for the remodelling of
English metres on the classic method. The notion was
not new. Ascham, in the *Schoolmaster*, pointed out "how
our English tongue in avoiding barbarous rhyming may
as well receive right quantity of syllables and true order
of versifying as either Greek or Latin, if a cunning
man have it in handling." He quoted Bishop Watson's
hexameters in proof of this proposition :—

"All travellers do gladly report great praise of Ulysses
For that he knew many men's manners and saw many cities."

Yet his good sense saved him from the absurdities into
which Stanyhurst, the translator of the *Aeneid*, fell when
he attempted Virgil in a "rude and beggarly" modern
imitation of the Latin rhythm. Ascham summed the
question up in a single sentence, prophetic of the future
course of English versification. "Although Carmen
Hexametrum doth rather trot and hobble than run
smoothly in our English tongue, yet I am sure our
English tongue will receive Carmen Iambicum as natur-
ally as either Greek or Latin." Harvey was not so finely
gifted as Ascham to perceive the native strength and
weakness of our language. He could see no reason why
the hexameter should not flourish, and wrote verses,
which, for grotesqueness, may pass muster with the most
"twitching and hopping" of their kind. Robert Greene,
who also tried his hand at the new style, composed
smoother but more insipid numbers in the eclogue of
Alexis. But Harvey, as I have said, exercised the influence of an imperious personality ; and one of his

friends was Edmund Spenser.   Through Harvey, Sidney
became acquainted with Spenser ; and it is well known
that the latter dedicated *The Shepherd's Kalendar* to him
in 1579.   The publication was anonymous.   The dedication ran as follows :—"To the noble and virtuous
gentleman, most worthy of all titles, both of learning
and chivalry, Master Philip Sidney."   The envoy opened
with these charming triplets :—

> " Go, little book ! thyself present,
> As child whose parent is unkent,
> To him that is the president
> Of nobleness and chivalry ;
> And if that envy bark at thee,
> As sure it will, for succour flee
> Under the shadow of his wing ;
> And, askèd who thee forth did bring,
> A shepherd's swain, say, did thee sing,
> All as his straying flock he fed ;
> And when his honour has thee read
> Crave pardon for thy hardihead."

In the midst, then, of his Court life Sidney made
friends with Harvey and with Spenser.   He associated
his dearer intimates, Fulke Greville and Edward Dyer,
in the same companionship.   And thus a little academy,
formed apparently upon the Italian model, came into
existence.   Its critical tendency was indicated by the
name Areopagus, given it perhaps in fun by Spenser ;
and its practical object was the reformation of English
poetry upon Italian and classical principles.   Unless I
am mistaken, no member of the club applied its doctrines
so thoroughly in practice as Sidney.   It is true that
Harvey wished to have it inscribed upon his grave that
he had fostered hexameters on English soil.   But in the

history of our poetical literature Harvey occupies no
place of honour. It is also true that Spenser elaborated
some lame hexameters. But his genius detected the
imposture; he wrote to Harvey, pointing out the insur-
mountable difficulties of English accent, and laughing at
the metre as being "either like a lame gosling that
draweth up one leg after, or like a lame dog that holdeth
one leg up."

Sidney, with his usual seriousness, took the search
after a reformed style of English poetry in earnest. He
made experiments in many kinds and various metres,
which are now preserved to us embedded in the text of
his *Arcadia*. Those poems form the most solid residuum
from the exercises of the Areopagus. They are not very
valuable; but they are interesting as showing what the
literary temper of England was, before the publication of
the *Faery Queen* and the overwhelming series of the
romantic dramas decided the fate of English poetry.
Like *Gorboduc* and other tragedies in the manner of
Seneca, these "reformed verses" were doomed to be
annihilated by the strong blast of the national genius.
But they have their importance for the student of cre-
puscular intervals between the darkness and the day-
spring; and it must not be forgotten that their author
did not intend them for the public eye. While studying
and using these verses as documents for the elucidation
of literary evolution, let us therefore bear in mind that
we are guilty of an indiscretion, and are prying on the
privacy of a gentleman who never sought the suffrage
of the vulgar.

It was at Wilton, then, in 1580, that Sidney began
the *Arcadia* in compliance with his sister's request.

The dedicatory epistle teaches us in what spirit we ought to approach the pages which he left unfinished, and which were given to the press after his decease :

" Here now have you, most dear, and most worthy to be most dear lady, this idle work of mine ; which, I fear, like the spider's web, will be thought fitter to be swept away than worn to any other purpose. For my part, in very truth, as the cruel fathers among the Greeks were wont to do to the babes they would not foster, I could well find it in my heart to cast out in some desert of forgetfulness this child which I am loth to father. But you desired me to do it, and your desire to my heart is an absolute commandment. Now it is done only for you, only to you. If you keep it to yourself, or to such friends who will weigh error in the balance of good-will, I hope for the father's sake it will be pardoned, perchance made much of, though in itself it have deformities. For, indeed, for severer eyes it is not, being a a trifle, and that triflingly handled."

These words were doubtless penned long after the first sheets of the *Arcadia*. That they were sincere is proved by Sidney's dying request to have the manuscript destroyed. He goes on to say that "his chief safety shall be the not walking abroad ; and his chief protection the using of your name, which, if much good-will do not deceive me, is worthy to be a sanctuary for a greater offender." We have, therefore, the strongest possible security that this famous *Arcadia* of Sir Philip Sidney, this " charm of ages," as Young pompously calls it, which passed through seventeen editions before 1674, was intended by its author only for his sister and a friendly circle. Yet, though we must approach it now like eavesdroppers, we may read in it, better perhaps than elsewhere, those tendencies of English literature which

were swallowed up and trampled over by the legionaries
of the great dramatic epoch.

It is not improbable that Lyly's *Euphues*, which first
saw the light in 1579, suggested to Sidney the notion of
writing a romance in a somewhat similar style. He did
not, however, catch the infection of Lyly's manner; and
the *Arcadia*, unlike *Euphues*, has no direct didactic purpose. Critics, soon after its appearance, imagined that
they could discern in its structure hidden references to
the main events of the age. But this may be considered
a delusion, based upon the prevalent tendency to seek
allegories in works of art and fancy—the tendency to
which Tasso bowed when he supplied a key to the
moralities of the *Gerusalemme*, and which induced
Spenser to read esoteric meanings into the *Orlando
Furioso*. Sidney had clearly in mind the *Arcadia* of
Sannazzaro; he also owed much to Montemayor's *Diana*
and the Greek romantic novelists. The style at first is
noticeably Italian, as will appear from certain passages
I mean to quote. After a while it becomes less idyllic
and ornate, and at last it merges into rapidity of narra-
tion. To sustain the manner of the earlier pages, which
remind us of Boccaccio and Sannazzaro, throughout the
labyrinthine intricacies of the fable, would have been
tedious. Perhaps, too, we may connect the alteration of
literary tone with Sidney's departure from Wilton to the
Court.

I shall not attempt a complete analysis of the *Arcadia*.
The main story is comparatively slender; but it is so
complicated by digressions and episodes that a full
account of the tangled plot would take up too much
space, and would undoubtedly prove wearisome to

modern readers.   Horace Walpole was not far wrong
when he asserted that "the patience of a young virgin in
love cannot now wade through" that jungle of pastoral,
sentimental, and heroical adventures.   A brief outline
of the tale, together with some specimens of Sidney's descriptive and sententious styles, must, however, here be
given, since it is not very likely that any readers of my
book will be impelled to turn the pages of the original.

Musidorus, Prince of Thessalia, and Pyrocles, Prince
of Macedon, were cousins.   An affection, such as bound
the knights of elder Greek romance together, united
them even more than the nearness of their blood.
Pyrocles, being the elder, taught his friend all that he
knew of good, and brave, and gracious.   Musidorus
learned willingly ; and thus the pair grew up to manhood in perfect love, twin flowers of gentleness and
chivalry.   When the story opens the two heroes have
just been wrecked on the Laconian coast.   A couple of
shepherds, Claius and Strephon, happened to be pacing
the seashore at that moment.   They noticed a young
man floating on a coffer, which the waves washed gradu-
ally landward.   He was "of so goodly shape and well-
pleasing favour that one would think death had in
him a lovely countenance ; and that, though he were
naked, nakedness was to him an apparel."   This youth
proved to be Musidorus.   Pyrocles meanwhile remained
upon the wreck ; and, while the shepherds were in the
act to rescue him, he was carried off by pirates under the
eyes of his sorrowing comrade.   There was nothing for
it but to leave him to his fate ; and Musidorus, after a
moment of wild despair, yielded to the exhortations of
the good shepherds, who persuaded him to journey with

them to the house of a just and noble gentleman named Kalander. The way was long; but, after two days' march, it brought them to Arcadia. The description of that land is justly celebrated.

"The third day after, in the time that the morning did strew roses and violets in the heavenly floor, against the coming of the sun, the nightingales (striving one with the other which could in most dainty variety recount their wrong-caused sorrow) made them put off their sleep; and rising from under a tree (which that night had been their pavilion), they went on their journey, which by-and-by welcomed Musidorus's eyes (wearied with the wasted soil of Laconia) with delightful prospects. There were hills which garnished their proud heights with stately trees: humble vallies, whose base estate seemed comforted with the refreshing of silver rivers: meadows enamelled with all sorts of eye-pleasing flowers; thickets, which being lined with most pleasant shade were witnessed so too by the cheerful disposition of many well-tuned birds; each pasture stored with sheep, feeding with sober security, while the pretty lambs with bleating outcry craved the dam's comfort: here a shepherd's boy piping, as though he should never be old: there a young shepherdess knitting, and withal singing; and it seemed that her voice comforted her hands to work, and her hands kept time to her voice-music. As for the houses of the country (for many houses came under their eye), they were all scattered, no two being one by the other, and yet not so far off as that it barred mutual succour; a show, as it were, of an accompanable solitariness and of a civil wildness."

In due course of time they arrived at the house of Kalander, where Musidorus was hospitably received.

"The house itself was built of fair and strong stone, not affecting so much any extraordinary kind of fineness as an honourable representing of a firm stateliness." "The servants not so many in number as cleanly in apparel and serviceable

in behaviour, testifying even in their countenances that their
master took as well care to be served as of them that did
serve."

Perhaps Sidney, when he penned these sentences,
thought of Penshurst. At any rate they remind us of
Jonson's lines upon that venerable country seat. The
pleasance, also, had the same charm of homeliness and
ancient peace :—

"The backside of the house was neither field, garden, nor
orchard ; or rather it was both field, garden, and orchard :
for as soon as the descending of the stairs had delivered them
down, they came into a place cunningly set with trees of the
most taste-pleasing fruits : but scarcely had they taken that
into their consideration, but that they were suddenly stepped
into a delicate green ; of each side of the green a thicket, and
behind the thickets again new beds of flowers, which being
under the trees, the trees were to them a pavilion, and they
to the trees a mosaical floor, so that it seemed that art therein would needs be delightful by counterfeiting his enemy
error and making order in confusion."

Here Musidorus sojourned some while, until he happened to hear that his host's son, Clitophon, had been
taken prisoner by the Helots, who were now in revolt
against their Laconian masters. Musidorus begged permission to go to the young man's rescue ; and when he
reached the rebels, he entered their walled city by a
stratagem and began a deadly battle in the market-place.
The engagement at first was general between the Helots
and the Arcadians, but at length it resolved itself into
a single combat, Musidorus attacking the leader of the
Helots with all his might. This duel remained for some
time equal and uncertain, when suddenly the brigand
chief threw down his sword, exclaiming, "What ! hath

Palladius forgotten the voice of Daiphantus?" It should
here be said that Pyrocles and Musidorus had agreed to
call each other by these assumed names. A joyful recognition of course ensued. Pyrocles related the series
of events by which he had been forced to head the rebels,
after being captured by them. Clitophon was released,
and all returned together to Arcadia.

At this point the love intrigue, which forms the main
interest of what Milton called "the vain amatorious poem
of Sir Philip Sidney's *Arcadia*," begins to unfold itself.
An eccentric sovereign, Basilius, Prince of Arcadia,
was married to an accomplished and beautiful woman,
Gynecia. They had two daughters, Pamela the elder,
and Philoclea the younger, equally matched in loveliness
of mind and person, yet differing by subtle contrasts
of their incomparable qualities. Basilius, in a fit of
jealousy and suspicion, had left his palace, and was now
residing with his wife and daughters in two rustic lodges,
deep-embowered by the forest. Gynecia, Philoclea, and
himself occupied one of these retreats. Pamela dwelt
in the other, under the care of a clownish peasant family,
consisting of Dametas, his hideous wife Miso, and their
still more odious daughter Mopsa. It need not be
related how Musidorus fell in love with Pamela and
Pyrocles with Philoclea. In order to be near the ladies
of their choice, the princes now assumed new names
and strange disguises. Pyrocles donned Amazon's attire
and called himself Zelmane. Musidorus became a shepherd and was known as Dorus. Both contrived to win
the affections of the princesses, but meanwhile they got
entangled in embarrassing and dangerous complications.
Dorus had to feign love for the disgusting Mopsa. Zel-

mane was persecuted by the passion of both Basilius and
Gynecia; Basilius deeming him a woman, Gynecia recognising a man through his disguise.   When Milton
condemned the *Arcadia* as " a book in that kind full
of mirth and witty, but among religious thoughts and
duties not worthy to be named, nor to be read at any
time without due caution," he was assuredly justified by
the unpleasant situation created for Zelmane.   A young
man, travestied as a girl, in love with a princess, and at
the same time harassed by the wanton solicitations of
both her father and her mother, is, to say the least, a
very risky subject for romance.   Yet Sidney treated it
with sufficient delicacy, and contrived in the end to
bring both Basilius and Gynecia to their senses.   "Loath-
somely loved and dangerously loving," Zelmane remained
long in this entanglement; but when he and Philoclea
eventually attained their felicity in marriage, both of
them concealed Gynecia's error.   And she "did, in the
remnant of her life, duly purchase [their good opinion]
with observing all duty and faith, to the example and
glory of Greece; so uncertain are mortal judgments, the
same person most infamous and most famous, and neither
justly."

I have dwelt on this part of the story because it an-
ticipates the plots of many Elizabethan dramas which
turned upon confusions of sex, and to which the custom
of boys acting female parts lent a curious complexity.
If space allowed I might also follow the more comic fortunes of Dorus, and show how the tale of Amphialus
(another lover of Philoclea) is interwoven with that of
Pyrocles and Musidorus.   This subordinate romance introduces one of the longest episodes of the work, when

Cecropia, the wicked mother of Amphialus, imprisons
Zelmane, Philoclea, and Pamela together in her castle.
It is during this imprisonment that Pamela utters the
prayer made famous by the fact that Charles I. is supposed to have used it just before his execution.   I will
quote it here at length, both for its beauty of style and
for the sake of this historical association :—

"O All-seeing Light and Eternal Life of all things, to
whom nothing is either so great that it may resist, or so
small that it is contemned ; look upon my misery with Thine
eye of mercy, and let Thine infinite power vouchsafe to limit
out some proportion of deliverance unto me, as to Thee shall
seem most convenient.   Let not injury, O Lord, triumph
over me, and let my faults by Thy hand be corrected, and
make not mine unjust enemy the minister of Thy justice.
But yet, my God, if, in Thy wisdom, this be the aptest
chastisement for my inexcusable folly, if this low bondage
be fitted for my over high desires, if the pride of my not
enough humble heart be thus to be broken, O Lord, I yield
unto Thy will, and joyfully embrace what sorrow Thou wilt
have me suffer.   Only thus much let me crave of Thee : let
my craving, O Lord, be accepted of Thee, since even that
proceeds from Thee ; let me crave, even by the noblest title
which in my greatest affliction I may give myself, that I am
Thy creature, and by Thy goodness, which is Thyself, that
Thou wilt suffer some beam of Thy majesty so to shine into
my mind that it may still depend confidently on Thee.   Let
calamity be the exercise, but not the overthrow of my virtue ;
let their power prevail, but prevail not to destruction.   Let
my greatness be their prey ; let my pain be the sweetness of
their revenge ; let them, if so it seem good unto Thee, vex
me with more and more punishment ; but, O Lord, let never
their wickedness have such a hand but that I may carry a
pure mind in a pure body."

Among the papers given to Bishop Juxon by Charles
upon the scaffold was this prayer, slightly altered in

some particulars. His enemies made it a cause of reproach against him, especially Milton, in a memorable passage of "Iconoclastes," from which I have already quoted certain phrases. "Who would have imagined," writes the Latin secretary, "so little fear in him of the true all-seeing Deity, so little reverence of the Holy Ghost, whose office it is to dictate and present our Christian prayers, so little care of truth in his last words, or honour to himself or to his friends, or sense of his afflictions, or that sad hour which was upon him, as immediately before his death to pop into the hand of that grave bishop who attended him, as a special relique of his saintly exercises, a prayer stolen word for word from the mouth of a heathen woman praying to a heathen god ; and that in no serious book, but in the vain amatorious poem of Sir Philip Sidney's *Arcadia ?* " Charles' defenders pointed out that the papers given to Juxon had been seized by the regicides, and accused them of foisting this prayer in on purpose to have the opportunity of traducing their victim to Puritan England. It is also noticeable that it does not appear in the first edition of *Eikon Basiliké,* nor in Dr. Earl's Latin version of that book. However the case may be, Dr. Johnson showed good sense when he wrote : "The use of it (the prayer) by adaptation was innocent ; and they who could so noisily censure it, with a little extension of their malice could contrive what they wanted to accuse."

Pamela's prayer has led me so far away from the intricacies of Sidney's *Arcadia* that I shall not return to further analyses of the fable. The chief merits of the book, as a whole, seem to be an almost inexhaustible variety of incidents, fairly correct character-drawing, purity of feeling, abundance of sententious maxims, and great richness of colouring in the descriptive passages. Its immense popularity may be ascribed to the fact that nothing exactly like it had appeared in English literature; for *Euphues* is by no means so romantically interesting or so varied in material, while the novels of Greene are both shorter and more monotonous. The chivalrous or heroic incidents are so well combined with the sentimental, and these again are so prettily set against the pastoral background, that, given an appetite for romance of the kind, each reader found something to stimulate his curiosity and to provide him with amusement. The defects of the *Arcadia* are apparent; as, for instance, its lack of humour, the extravagance of many of its situations, the whimsicality of its conceits, and the want of solid human realism in its portraits. These defects were, however, no bar to its popularity in the sixteenth century; nor would they count as such at present were it not, as Dr. Zouch pertinently remarks, that "the taste, the manners, the opinions, the language of the English nation, have undergone a very great revolution since the reign of Queen Elizabeth." Such a revolution condemns all works of prose fiction which fascinated a bygone age, and which are not kept alive by humour and by solid human realism, to ever-gradually-deepening oblivion.

Before concluding this chapter there is another point of view under which the *Arcadia* must be considered. Sidney interspersed its prose with verses, after the model of Sannazzaro's pastoral, sometimes introducing them as occasion suggested into the mouths of his chief personages, and sometimes making them the subject of poetical disputes between the shepherds of the happy

country. Some of these poems are among the best which
he composed. I would cite in particular the beautiful
sonnet which begins and ends with this line: "My true
love hath my heart, and I have his;" and another
opening with—"Beauty hath force to catch the human
sight." But what gives special interest to the verses
scattered over the pages of *Arcadia* is that in a large
majority of them Sidney put in practice the theories of
the Areopagus. Thus we have English hexameters,
elegiacs, sapphics, phaleuciacs or hendecasyllables, asclepiads, and anacreontics. I will present some specimens
of each. Here then are hexameters :—

> "Lady reserved by the heavens to do pastors' company
>   honour,
> Joining your sweet voice to the rural muse of a desert,
> Here you fully do find this strange operation of love,
> How to the woods love runs as well as rides to the palace;
> Neither he bears reverence to a prince nor pity to beggar,
> But (like a point in midst of a circle) is still of a nearness.
> All to a lesson he draws, neither hills nor caves can avoid
>   him."

One elegiac couplet will suffice :—

> "Fortune, Nature, Love, long have contended about me,
>   Which should most miseries cast on a worm that
>   I am."

Nor will it be needful to quote more than one sapphic
stanza :—

> "If mine eyes can speak to do hearty errand,
> Or mine eyes' language she do hap to judge of,
> So that eyes' message be of her receivèd,
>   Hope, we do live yet."

The hendecasyllables, though comparatively easy to

write in English, hobble in a very painful manner, as
thus :—

> " Reason, tell me thy mind, if here be reason,
>   In this strange violence to make resistance,
>   Where sweet graces erect the stately banner
>   Of virtue's regiment, shining in harness."

So do the asclepiads, which, however, are by no means
so easy of execution :—

> "O sweet woods, the delight of solitariness !
>   O how much I do like your solitariness !
>   Where man's mind hath a freed consideration
>   Of goodness to receive lovely direction ;
>   Where senses do behold the order of heavenly host,
>   And wise thoughts do behold what the Creator is."

The anacreontics, being an iambic measure, come off
somewhat better, as may be judged by this transcript
from a famous fragment of Sappho :—

> " My Muse, what ails this ardour ?
>   Mine eyes be dim, my limbs shake,
>   My voice is hoarse, my throat scorched,
>   My tongue to this my roof cleaves,
>   My fancy amazed, my thoughts dulled,
>   My heart doth ache, my life faints,
>   My soul begins to take leave."

It is obvious from these quotations that what the
school called " our rude and beggarly rhyming " is not
only more natural, but also more artistic than their
" reformed verse." Indeed, it may be said without
reserve that Sidney's experiments in classical metres have
no poetical value whatsoever. They are only interesting
as survivals from an epoch when the hexameter seemed
to have an equal chance of survival with the decasyllabic

unrhymed iambic. The same is true about many of
Sidney's attempts to acclimatise Italian forms of verse.
Thus we find imbedded in the *Arcadia* terza rima and
ottava rima, sestines and madrigals, a canzone in which
the end of each line rhymes with a syllable in the middle
of the next.   So conscientious was he in the attempt to
reproduce the most difficult Italian metres that he even
attempted terza rima with *sdrucciolo* or trisyllabic rhymes.
I will select an example :—

> " If sunny beams shame heavenly habitation,
>   If three-leaved grass seem to the sheep unsavory,
>   Then base and sore is Love's most high vocation.
>   Or if sheep's cries can help the sun's own bravery,
>   Then may I hope my pipe may have ability
>   To help her praise who decks me in her slavery."

But enough of this. It has proved a difficult task to
introduce terza rima at all into English literature ; to
make so exceptionally exacting a species of it as the
sdrucciolo at all attractive, would almost be beyond the
powers of Mr. Swinburne. The octave, as handled by
Sidney, is passable, as will appear from the even flow of
this stanza :—

> " While thus they ran a low but levelled race,
>   While thus they lived (this was indeed a life !)
>   With nature pleased, content with present case,
>   Free of proud fears, brave beggary, smiting strife
>   Of clime-fall court, the envy-hatching place,
>   While those restless desires in great men rife
>   To visit folks so low did much disdain,
>   This while, though poor, they in themselves did reign."

Of the sestines I will not speak. That form has
always seemed to me tedious even in the hands of the

most expert Italian masters; and Sidney was not the
sort of poet to add grace to its formality by any spright-
liness of treatment. It should be noticed that some of
the songs in the *Arcadia* are put into the mouth of a sad
shepherd who is Sidney himself. Phillisides (for so he
has chosen to Latinise the first syllables of his Christian
and surnames) appears late in the romance, and prepares
us to expect the higher poetry of *Astrophel and Stella*.

CHAPTER V

LIFE AT COURT AGAIN, AND MARRIAGE

WHILE Philip was in retirement at Wilton two events of interest happened. His nephew, William Herbert, saw the light upon the 28th of April; and Edmund Spenser left England for Ireland as secretary to the new Viceroy, Lord Grey of Wilton. The birth of the future Earl of Pembroke forcibly reminds us of Sidney's position in the history of English literature. This baby in the cradle was destined to be Shakespeare's friend and patron; possibly also to inspire the sonnets which a publisher inscribed in Shakespeare's name to Master W. H. We are wont to regard those enigmatical compositions as the product of Shakespeare's still uncertain manhood. But William Herbert was yet a child when his uncle Philip's life-work ended. *Astrophel and Stella* had circulated among its author's private friends for at least four years when Zutphen robbed England of her poet-hero. At that date little Herbert, for whom Shakespeare subsequently wrote the lines—

> "Take all my loves, my love, yea, take them all;
> What hast thou then more than thou hadst before?"—

this little Herbert was but in his seventh year.

It is also possible, but not probable, that, while Philip was away in Wiltshire, his half-affianced bride, the daughter of the Earl of Essex, gave her hand to another suitor. Her guardian, the Earl of Huntingdon, wrote upon the 10th of March, in 1580, to Lord Burleigh, that he considered Lord Rich "a proper gentleman, and one in years very fit for my Lady Penelope Devereux, if, with the favour and liking of her Majesty, the matter might be brought to pass." Lord Rich certainly married Penelope Devereux; but whether it was in 1580, or rather in 1581, admits of discussion. To fix the exact date of her betrothal is a matter of some moment. I must therefore point out that, at that time in England, the commencement of the year dated officially from March 25. In private correspondence, however, the 1st of January had already begun to mark the opening of a new year. Privately, then, Lord Huntingdon's letter may have carried the date, 1580, as we understand it; but, officially, it must have been reckoned into the year which we call 1581. Now this letter is endorsed by Burleigh or his secretary, officially, under the year 1580; and, therefore, we have a strong presumption in favour of Penelope's not having been engaged to Lord Rich until 1581, seeing that the month of March in 1580 counted then for our month of March in 1581. When I review *Astrophel and Stella* it will appear that I do not attach very great importance to this question of dates. But I think it safer, on the evidence, to place Stella's marriage in the spring or summer of 1581.

Lord Rich was the son of the Lord Chancellor of England, who had lately died, bequeathing to his heir a very substantial estate, and a large portion of his own

coarse temperament. If we may trust the Earl of
Devonshire's emphatic statement, made some twenty-five
years later to King James, this marriage was not to
the mind of the lady. He says that Penelope, "being
in the power of her friends, was married against her will
unto one against whom she did protest at the solemnity
and ever after ; between whom, from the very first day,
there ensued continual discord, although the same fears
that forced her to marry constrained her to live with
him." I may here remind my readers of her subsequent
history. During her husband's lifetime she left him and
became the mistress of Sir Charles Blount, to whom she
bore three children out of wedlock. He advanced to
the peerage with the inherited title of Lord Mountjoy,
and was later on created Earl of Devonshire ; while
Lady Rich, in spite of her questionable conduct, received, by patent, the dignity and precedence of the
most ancient Earldom of Essex. Having been divorced
from Lord Rich, she was afterwards at liberty to marry
her lover ; and in 1605 she became the Countess of
Devonshire. James refused to countenance the nuptials.
He had tolerated the previous illicit connection. But his
opinions upon divorce made him regard its legalisation
with indignant horror. Stella died in 1607 a disgraced
woman, her rights of wifehood and widowhood remaining unrecognised.

In the course of the summer (1580), Leicester left his
retirement and returned to Court. It was understood
that though still not liking the French match, he would
in future offer no opposition to the queen's wishes ; and
on these terms he induced Philip also to make his
peace with her Majesty. We find him, accordingly,

again in London before the autumn.   Two of the longest
private letters from his pen may be referred to this period.
They are addressed to his brother Robert Sidney, who
afterwards became Lord Leicester.   This young man was
then upon his travels, spending more money than his
father's distressed circumstances could well afford.
Philip sent him supplies, using language of great delicacy
and warm brotherly affection: "For the money you
have received, assure yourself (for it is true) there is
nothing I spend so pleaseth me, as that which is for you.
If ever I have ability, you will find it ; if not, yet shall
not any brother living be better beloved than you of me."
"For £200 a year, assure yourself, if the estates of
England remain, you shall not fail of it ; use it to your
best profit."   Where Philip found the money may be
wondered ; but that he gave it with good grace is un-
questionable.   Probably he received more from the
queen in allowances than we are aware of; for he
ranked among the favoured courtiers then known as
"pensioners."   As was the fashion of those times, he
lectured his brother somewhat pompously on how to use
the opportunities of the grand tour.   Robert was con-
stantly to observe the "virtue, passion, and vices" of
the foreign countries through which he travelled.

"Even in the Kingdom of China, which is almost as far
as the Antipodes from us, their good laws and customs are to
be learned ; but to know their riches and power is of little
purpose for us, since that can neither advance nor hinder us.
But in our neighbour countries, both these things are to be
marked, as well the latter, which contain things for themselves, as the former, which seek to know both those, and
how their riches and power may be to us available, or otherwise.   The countries fittest for both these are those you are

going into. France is above all other most needful for us to mark, especially in the former kind ; next is Spain and the Low Countries ; then Germany, which in my opinion excels all others as much in the latter consideration, as the other doth in the former, yet neither are void of neither ; for as Germany, methinks, doth excel in good laws, and well administering of justice, so are we likewise to consider in it the many princes with whom we may have league, the places of trade, and means to draw both soldiers and furniture thence in time of need. So on the other side, as in France and Spain, we are principally to mark how they stand towards us both in power and inclination ; so are they not without good and fitting use, even in the generality of wisdom to be known. As in France, the courts of parliament, their subaltern jurisdiction, and their continual keeping of paid soldiers. In Spain, their good and grave proceedings ; their keeping so many provinces under them, and by what manner, with the true points of honour ; wherein since they have the most open conceit, if they seem over curious, it is an easy matter to cut off when a man sees the bottom. Flanders likewise, besides the neighbourhood with us, and the annexed considerations thereunto, hath divers things to be learned, especially their governing their merchants and other trades. Also for Italy, we know not what we have, or can have, to do with them, but to buy their silks and wines ; and as for the other point, except Venice, whose good laws and customs we can hardly proportion to ourselves, because they are quite of a contrary government ; there is little there but tyrannous oppression, and servile yielding to them that have little or no right over them. And for the men you shall have there, although indeed some be excellently learned, yet are they all given to counterfeit learning, as a man shall learn among them more false grounds of things than in any place else that I know ; for from a tapster upwards, they are all discoursers in certain matters and qualities, as horsemanship, weapons, painting, and such are better there than in other countries ; but for other matters, as well, if not better, you shall have them in nearer places."

The second of the two epistles (dated from Leicester

House, Oct. 18, 1580), contains more personal matter. "Look to your diet, sweet Robin," he says, "and hold up your heart in courage and virtue; truly great part of my comfort is in you." And again: "Now, sweet brother, take a delight to keep and increase your music; you will not believe what a want I find of it in my melancholy times." It appears, then, that Philip, unlike many gentlemen of that age, could not touch the lute or teach the "saucy jacks" of the virginal to leap in measure. Then follows another bit of playful exhortation: "I would by the way your worship would learn a better hand; you write worse than I, and I write evil enough; once again have a care of your diet, and consequently of your complexion; remember *Gratior est veniens in pulchro corpore virtus.*" If Ben Jonson was right in what he said of Philip's complexion, this advice had its ground in tiresome experience. On the subject of manly exercises he has also much to say: "At horsemanship, when you exercise it, read Crison Claudio, and a book that is called *La Gloria del Cavallo*, withal that you may join the thorough contemplation of it with the exercise; and so shall you profit more in a month than others in a year; and mark the bitting, saddling, and curing of horses."

"When you play at weapons, I would have you get thick caps and brasers, and play out your play lustily, for indeed ticks and dalliances are nothing in earnest, for the time of the one and the other greatly differs; and use as well the blow as the thrust; it is good in itself, and besides exerciseth your breath and strength, and will make you a strong man at the tourney and barriers. First, in any case practise the single sword, and then with the dagger; let no day pass without an hour or two such exercise; the rest study, or confer diligently, and so shall you come home to my comfort and credit."

Studies come in for their due share of attention. "Take delight likewise in the mathematicals; Mr. Savile is excellent in them. I think you understand the sphere; if you do, I care little for any more astronomy in you. Arithmetic and geometry I would wish you were well seen in, so as both in matters of number and measure you might have a feeling and active judgment. I would you did bear the mechanical instruments, wherein the Dutch excel." It may be said with reference to this paragraph that Mr. Savile was Robert Sidney's travelling governor. The sphere represented medieval astronomy. Based upon the traditional interpretation of the Ptolemaic doctrine, it lent itself to theoretical disquisitions upon cosmology in general, as well as to abstruse speculations regarding the locality of paradise and heaven, the elements, and superhuman existences. On the point of style Philip observes : "So you can speak and write Latin, not barbarously, I never require great study in Ciceronianism, the chief abuse of Oxford, *qui dum verba sectantur res ipsas negligunt.*" History being Robert Sidney's favourite study, his brother discourses on it more at large.

I have quoted thus liberally from Philip's letters to Robert Sidney, because of the agreeable light they cast upon his character. It is clear they were not penned for perusal by the public. "My eyes are almost closed up, overwatched with tedious business," says the writer; and his last words are, "Lord ! how I have babbled." Yet, though hastily put together, and somewhat incoherently expressed, the thoughts are of excellent pith, and one

passage upon history, in particular, reads like a rough sketch for part of the "Defence of Poesy."

After weighing the unaffected words of brotherly counsel and of affectionate interest which Philip sent across the sea to Robert, we are prepared for Sir Henry Sidney's warm panegyric of his first-born to his second son. He had indeed good hopes of Robert; but he built more on Philip, as appears from the following sentence in a letter to Sir Francis Walsingham : " I having three sons, one of excellent good proof, the second of great good proof, and the third not to be despaired of, but very well to be liked." Therefore he frequently exhorted Robert to imitate the qualities of his "best brother." " *Perge, perge*, my Robin, in the filial fear of God, and in the meanest imagination of yourself, and to the loving direction of your most loving brother. Imitate his virtues, exercises, studies, and actions. He is the rare ornament of this age, the very formular that all well disposed young gentlemen of our Court do form also their manners and life by. In truth I speak it without flattery of him or of myself ; he hath the most rare virtues that ever I found in any man. Once again I say imitate him." And once more, at a later date : "Follow your discreet and virtuous brother's rule, who with great discretion, to his great commendation, won love, and could variously ply ceremony with ceremony."

The last extant letter of Languet to Philip was written in October of this year. The old man congratulates his friend upon returning to the Court; but he adds a solemn warning against its idleness and dissipations. Familiarity with English affairs confirmed his bad opinion of Elizabeth's Court circle. He saw that

she was arbitrary in her distribution of wealth and honours ; he feared lest Philip's merits should be ignored, while some more worthless favourite was being pampered. Once he had hoped that his service of the queen would speedily advance him to employment in public affairs. Now he recognised the possibility of that young hopeful life being wasted upon formalities and pastimes ; and for England he prophesied a coming time of factions, complicated by serious foreign troubles. It is the letter of a saddened man, slowly declining towards the grave, amid forebodings which the immediate future of Europe only too well justified. Languet had now just eleven months more to live. He died in September 1581 at Antwerp, nursed through his last illness by the wife of his noble friend Philip du Plessis Mornay, and followed to the tomb by William, Prince of Orange. Among the poems given to Phillisides in the *Arcadia* is one which may perhaps have been written about the time when Languet's death had brought to Philip's memory the debt of gratitude he owed this faithful counsellor :—

> " The song I sang old Languet had me taught,
>   Languet the shepherd best swift Ister knew
> For clerkly reed, and hating what is naught,
>   For faithful heart, clean hands, and mouth as true ;
>   With his sweet skill my skilless youth he drew
> To have a feeling taste of Him that sits
> Beyond the heaven, far more beyond our wits.

> " He said the music best thilk powers pleased
>   Was sweet accord between our wit and will,
> Where highest notes to godliness are raised,
>   And lowest sink not down to jot of ill ;
>   With old true tales he wont mine ears to fill,
> How shepherds did of yore, how now they thrive,
> Spoiling their flocks, or while 'twixt them they strive.

"He likèd me, but pitied lustful youth ;
   His good strong staff my slippery years upbore ;
He still hoped well because I lovèd truth ;
   Till forced to part, with heart and eyes even sore,
   To worthy Corydon he gave me o'er."

On New Year's Day, 1581, Philip presented the
queen with a heart of gold, a chain of gold, and a whip
with a golden handle.   These gifts symbolised his devo-
tion to her, and her right to chastise him.   The year is
marked in his biography by his first entrance into Parliament, as knight of the shire for Kent.   He only sat two
months; but during that short period he joined the
committees appointed to frame rules for enforcing
laws against Catholics, and for suppressing seditious
practices by word or deed against her Majesty.   The
French match was still uppermost in Elizabeth's mind.
She hankered after it ; and some of the wisest heads in
Europe, among them William the Silent, approved of
the project.   Yet she was unable to decide.   The Duke
of Anjou had raised questions as to the eventuality of
England becoming dependent on the French Crown ;
which it might have been, if he had married the Queen,
and succeeded to his childless brother.   This made her
pause and reflect.   She was, moreover, debating the
scheme of an alliance with Henri III. against Spain.
Between the two plans her mind wavered.   As Walsingham wrote to Burleigh: "When her Majesty is pressed
to the marriage, then she seemeth to affect a league ;
and when the league is yielded to, then she liketh better
a marriage ; and when thereupon she is moved to assent
to marriage, then she hath recourse to the league ; and
when the motion is for the league, or any request is

made for money, then her Majesty returneth to the
marriage."

These hesitations seem to have been augmented by
the urgency of the French Court.   On the 16th of April
Francis of Bourbon arrived from Paris at the head of
a magnificent embassy, with the avowed object of settling
preliminaries.   They were received with due honour by
the principle nobles of Elizabeth's Court, all open opposition to the marriage having now been withdrawn by
common consent.   Among the entertainments provided
for the envoys during their sojourn in London, Philip
played a conspicuous part.   Together with the Earl of
Arundel, Lord Windsor, and Fulke Greville, he prepared
a brilliant display of chivalry.   Calling themselves the
Four Foster Children of Desire, they pledged their word
to attack and win, if possible, by force of arms, the
Fortress of Perfect Beauty.   This fort, which was understood to be the allegorical abode of the queen, was
erected in the Tilt Yard at Whitehall.   Seven times
the number of the challengers, young gentlemen of
knightly prowess, offered themselves as defenders of the
fortress; and it was quite clear from the first how the
tournament would end.   This foregone conclusion did
not, however, mar the sport; and the compliment intended to Elizabeth would have been spoiled, if the Foster
Children of Desire could have forced their way into her
Castle of Beauty.   The assault upon the Fortress of
Perfect Beauty began on the 15th of May and was continued on the 16th, when the challengers acknowledged
their defeat.   They submitted their capitulation to the
queen, by the mouth of a lad, attired in ash-coloured
clothes, and bearing an olive-branch.   From the detailed

accounts which survive of the event, I will only transcribe
what serves to bring Philip Sidney and his train before
us. The passage describes his entrance on the first day
of the lists :—

"Then proceeded Master Philip Sidney in very sumptuous manner, with armour, part blue and the rest gilt and
engraven, with four spare horses, having caparisons and
furniture very rich and costly, as some of cloth of gold
embroidered with pearl, and some embroidered with gold
and silver feathers, very richly and cunningly wrought. He
had four pages that rode on his four spare horses, who had
cassock coats and Venetian hose, all of cloth of silver, laied
with gold lace, and hats of the same with gold bands and
white feathers, and each one a pair of white buskins. Then
had he thirty gentlemen and yeomen, and four trumpeters,
who were all in cassock coats and Venetian hose of yellow
velvet laied with silver lace, yellow velvet caps with silver
bands and white feathers, and every one a pair of white
buskins ; and they had upon their coats a scroll or band of
silver, which came scarf-wise over the shoulder, and so down
under the arm, with this posy or sentence written upon it,
both before and behind : *Sic nos non nobis.*"

It behoves us not to ask, but we cannot help wondering, where the money came from for this costly show.
Probably Philip was getting into debt. His appeals to
friends with patronage at their disposal became urgent
during the ensuing months. Though he obtained no
post which combined public duties with pay, a sinecure
worth £120 a year was given him. It must be said to
his credit that he did not so much desire unearned
money as some lucrative appointment, entailing labour
and responsibility. This the queen would not grant ;
even an application made by him so late as the summer
of 1583, begging for employment at the Ordnance under

his uncle Warwick, was refused. Meanwhile his European reputation brought invitations, which prudence
bade him reject. One of these arrived from Don
Antonio of Portugal, a bastard pretender to that kingdom, calling upon Philip Sidney to join his forces.
The life at Court, onerous by reason of its expenditure,
tedious through indolence and hope deferred, sweetened
chiefly by the companionship of Greville and Dyer, wore
tiresomely on. And over all these months wavered the
fascinating vision of Stella, now a wife, to whom
Phillisides was paying ardent homage. It may well be
called a dangerous passage in his short life, the import
of which we shall have to fathom when we take up *Astrophel and Stella* for perusal. Courtly monotony had its
distractions. The French match, for instance, afforded
matter for curiosity and mild excitement. This reached
its climax when the Duke of Anjou arrived in person.
He came in November, and stayed three months. When
he left England in February 1582, the world knew that
this project of a marriage for Elizabeth was at an end.
Sidney, with the flower of English aristocracy, attended
the French prince to Antwerp. There he was pro-
claimed Duke of Brabant, and welcomed with shows of
fantastic magnificence. We may dismiss all further
notice of him from the present work, with the mention
of his death in 1584. It happened on the first of June,
preceding the Prince of Orange's assassination by just
one month. People thought that Anjou also had been
murdered.

The greater part of the year 1582 is a blank in
Philip's biography. We only know that he was frequently absent from the Court, and in attendance on his

father. Sir Henry Sidney's affairs were seriously involved. The Crown refused him substantial aid, and kept him to his post at Ludlow Castle. Yet, at the beginning of 1583, we find Philip again in waiting on the queen; presenting her with a golden flower-pot, and receiving the gracious gift of a lock of the royal virgin's hair. In January Prince Casimir had to be installed Knight of the Garter. Philip was chosen as his proxy, and obtained the honour of knighthood for himself. Henceforward he takes rank as Sir Philip Sidney of Penshurst.

Never thoroughly at ease in courtly idleness, Philip formed the habit of turning his eyes westward, across the ocean, towards those new continents where wealth and boundless opportunities of action lay ready for adventurous knights. Frobisher's supposed discovery of gold in 1577 drew an enthusiastic letter from him. In 1578 he was meditating some "Indian project." In 1580 he wrote wistfully to his brother Robert about Drake's return, "of which yet I know not the secret points; but about the world he hath been, and rich he is returned." In 1582 his college friend, Richard Hakluyt, inscribed the first collection of his *Voyages* with Sidney's name. All things pointed in the direction of his quitting England for the New World, if a suitable occasion should present itself, and if the queen should grant him her consent. During the spring of 1583 projects for colonisation, or plantation as it then was termed, were afloat among the west country gentlefolk. Sir Humphrey Gilbert and his half-brother Walter Raleigh, with Sir George Peckham and others, thought of renewing the attempts they had already made in

1578. Elizabeth in that year had signed her first charter of lands to be explored beyond the seas, in favour of Sir Humphrey Gilbert; and now she gave a second to Sir Philip Sidney. It licensed and authorised him

"To discover, search, find out, view, and inhabit certain parts of America not yet discovered, and out of those countries, by him, his heirs, factors, or assignees, to have and enjoy, to him, his heirs, and assignees for ever, such and so much quantity of ground as shall amount to the number of thirty hundred thousand acres of ground and wood, with all commodities, jurisdictions, and royalties, both by sea and land, with full power and authority that it should and might be lawful for the said Sir Philip Sidney, his heirs and assignees, at all times thereafter to have, take, and lead in the same voyage, to travel thitherwards or to inhabit there with him or them, and every or any of them, such and so many her Majesty's subjects as should willingly accompany him and them and every or any of them, with sufficient shipping and furniture for their transportation."

In other words, her Majesty granted to Sir Philip Sidney the pretty little estate of three millions of acres in North America. It is true that the land existed, so to say, *in nubibus*, and was by no means sure to prove an El Dorado. It was far more sure that if the grantee got possession of it, he would have to hold it by his own strength; for Britain, at this epoch, was not pledged to support her colonies. Yet considering the present value of the soil in Virginia or New England, the mere fantastic row of seven figures in American acres, so lightly signed away by her Majesty, is enough to intoxicate the imagination. How Philip managed to extort or wheedle this charter from Elizabeth we have no means of knowing. She was exceedingly jealous of her courtiers, and would not willingly lose sight of them. When Philip two years later engaged himself in a colonising expedition, we shall see that she positively forbade him to leave England. Now, however, it is probable she knew that he could not take action on her gift. She was merely bestowing an interest in specula- tions which cost her nothing and might bring him profit. At any rate, the matter took this turn. In July 1583 he executed a deed relinquishing 30,000 acres, together with "all royalties, titles, pre-eminences, privileges, liberties, and dignities," which the queen's grant carried, to his friend Sir George Peckham.

The reason of this act of resignation was that Philip had pledged his hand in marriage to Frances, daughter of Sir Francis Walsingham. So far back as December 1581 there are indications that his friendship with Walsingham and his family was ripening into something more intimate. We do not know the date of his marriage for certain; but it is probable that he was already a husband before the month of July.

A long letter addressed in March 1583 by Sir Henry Sidney to Walsingham must here be used, since it throws the strongest light upon the circumstances of the Sidney family, and illustrates Sir Henry's feeling with regard to his son's marriage. The somewhat dis- contented tone which marks its opening is, I think, rather apologetical than regretful. Sir Henry felt that, on both sides, the marriage was hardly a prudent one. He had expected some substantial assistance from the Crown through Walsingham's mediation. This had not been granted; and he took the opportunity of again laying a succinct report of his past services and present

necessities before the secretary of state, in the hope
that something might yet be done to help him. The
document opens as follows :—

"DEAR SIR—I have understood of late that coldness is
thought in me in proceeding in the matter of marriage of
our children. In truth, sir, it is not so, nor so shall it ever
be found ; for compremitting the consideration of the articles
to the Earls named by you, and to the Earl of Huntingdon,
I most willingly agree, and protest, and joy in the alliance
with all my heart. But since, by your letters of the 3d of
January, to my great discomfort I find there is no hope of
relief of her Majesty for my decayed estate in her Highness'
service, I am the more careful to keep myself able, by sale
of part of that which is left, to ransom me out of the servitude I live in for my debts ; for as I know, sir, that it is
the virtue which is, or that you suppose is, in my son, that
you made choice of him for your daughter, refusing haply
far greater and far richer matches than he, so was my confidence great that by your good means I might have obtained
some small reasonable suit of her Majesty ; and therefore
I nothing regarded any present gain, for if I had, I might
have received a great sum of money for my good will of my
son's marriage, greatly to the relief of my private biting
necessity."

After this exordium, Sir Henry takes leave to review
his actions as Viceroy of Ireland and Governor of Wales,
with the view of showing how steadfastly he had served
his queen and how ill he had been recompensed.

"Three times her Majesty hath sent me her Deputy into
Ireland, and in every of the three times I sustained a great
and a violent rebellion, every one of which I subdued, and
(with honourable peace) left the country in quiet. I returned
from each of these three Deputations three hundred pounds
worse than I went."

It would be impertinent to the subject of this essay

were I to follow Sir Henry in the minute and interesting account of his Irish administration. Suffice it to say that the letter to Walsingham is both the briefest and the most material statement of facts which we possess regarding that period of English rule. Omitting then all notice of public affairs, I pass on to confidences of a more personal character. After dwelling upon sundry embassies and other employments, he proceeds :—

" Truly, sir, by all these I neither won nor saved ; but now, by your patience, once again to my great and high office—for great it is in that in some sort I govern the third part of this realm under her most excellent Majesty ; high it is, for by that I have precedency of great personages and far my betters : happy it is for the people whom I govern, as before is written, and most happy for the commodity that I have by the authority of that place to do good every day, if I have grace, to one or other; wherein I confess I feel no small felicity ; but for any profit I gather by it, God and the people (seeing my manner of life) knoweth it is not possible how I should gather any.

" For, alas, sir! how can I, not having one groat of pension belonging to the office? I have not so much ground as will feed a mutton. I sell no justice, I trust you do not hear of any order taken by me ever reversed, nor my name or doings in any court ever brought in question. And if my mind were so base and contemptible as I would take money of the people whom I command for my labour taken among them, yet could they give me none, or very little, for the causes that come before me are causes of people mean, base, and many very beggars. Only £20 a week to keep an honourable house, and 100 marks a year to bear foreign charges, I have ; . . . but true books of account shall be, when you will, showed unto you that I spend above £30 a week. Here some may object that I upon the same keep my wife and her followers. True it is she is now with me, and hath been this half year, and before not in many years ; and if both she and I had our food and house-room free, as we have not, in my conscience we have deserved it. For my part, I am not idle, but every day I work in my function; and she, for her old service, and marks yet remaining in her face taken in the same, meriteth her meat. When I went to Newhaven I left her a full fair lady, in mine eye at least the fairest; and when I returned I found her as foul a lady as the small-pox could make her, which she did take by continual attendance of her Majesty's most precious person (sick of the same disease), the scars of which, to her resolute discomfort, ever since have done and doth remain in her face, so as she liveth solitarily, *sicut nicticorax in domicilio suo*, more to my charge than if we had boarded together, as we did before that evil accident happened."

The epistle ends with a general review of Sir Henry's pecuniary situation, by which it appears that the Sidney estate had been very considerably impoverished during his tenure of it.

"The rest of my life is with an over-long precedent discourse manifested to you. But this to your little comfort I cannot omit, that whereas my father had but one son, and he of no great proof, being of twenty-four years of age at his death, and I having three sons; one of excellent good proof, the second of great good proof, and the third not to be despaired of, but very well to be liked; if I die to-morrow next I should leave them worse than my father left me by £20,000; and I am now fifty-four years of age, toothless and trembling, being £5000 in debt, yea, and £30,000 worse than I was at the death of my most dear king and master, King Edward VI.

"I have not of the crown of England of my own getting, so much ground as I can cover with my foot. All my fees amount not to 100 marks a year. I never had since the queen's reign any extraordinary aid by license, forfeit, or otherwise. And yet for all that was done, and somewhat more than here is written, I cannot obtain to have in fee-farm £100 a year, already in my own possession, paying the rent.

"And now, dear sir and brother, an end of this tragical

discourse, tedious for you to read, but more tedious it would
have been if it had come written with my own hand, as first
it was. Tragical I may well term it: for that it began with
the joyful love and great liking with likelihood of matri-
monial match between our most dear and sweet children
(whom God bless), and endeth with declaration of my unfortunate and hard estate.

"Our Lord bless you with long life and happiness. I
pray you, sir, commend me most heartily to my good lady,
cousin, and sister, your wife, and bless and kiss our sweet
daughter. And if you will vouchsafe, bestow a blessing upon
the young knight, Sir Philip."

There is not much to say of Philip's bride. He and
she lived together as man and wife barely three years.
Nothing remains to prove that she was either of assistance to him or the contrary. After his death she contracted a secret marriage with Robert Devereux, the Earl
of Essex; and when she lost this second husband on the
scaffold, she adopted the Catholic religion and became the
wife of Lord Clanricarde. In this series of events I can
see nothing to her discredit, considering the manners
of that century. Her daughter by Philip, it is known,
made a brilliant marriage with the Earl of Rutland.
Her own repeated nuptials may be taken to prove her
personal attractiveness. Sir Philip Sidney, who must
have been intimately acquainted with her character,
chose her for his wife while his passion for Penelope
Devereux had scarcely cooled; and he did so without
the inducements which wealth or brilliant fortunes might
have offered.

CHAPTER VI

"ASTROPHEL AND STELLA"

AMONG Sidney's miscellaneous poems there is a lyric, which has been supposed, not without reason, I think, to express his feelings upon the event of Lady Penelope Devereux's marriage to Lord Rich.

"Ring out your bells, let mourning shows be spread;
  For Love is dead:
    All love is dead, infected
  With plague of deep disdain:
    Worth, as naught worth, rejected,
  And faith fair scorn doth gain.
      From so ungrateful fancy,
      From such a female frenzy,
      From them that use men thus,
      Good Lord, deliver us!

"Weep, neighbours, weep; do you not hear it said
  That Love is dead?
    His death-bed, peacock's folly;
  His winding-sheet is shame;
    His will, false-seeming holy;
  His sole executor, blame.
      From so ungrateful fancy,
      From such a female frenzy,
      From them that use men thus,
      Good Lord, deliver us!

> " Alas ! I lie : rage hath this error bred ;
>   Love is not dead ;
>   Love is not dead, but sleepeth
>   In her unmatchèd mind,
>   Where she his counsel keepeth
>   Till due deserts she find.
>   Therefore from so vile fancy,
>   To call such wit a frenzy,
>   Who Love can temper thus,
>   Good Lord, deliver us !"

These stanzas sufficiently set forth the leading passion
of *Astrophel and Stella.*   That series of poems celebrates
Sir Philip Sidney's love for Lady Rich after her marriage,
his discovery that this love was returned, and the curb
which her virtue set upon his too impetuous desire.
Before the publication of Shakespeare's sonnets, these
were undoubtedly the finest love poems in our language ; and though exception may be taken to the fact
that they were written for a married woman, their purity
of tone and philosophical elevation of thought separate
them from the vulgar herd of amatorious verses.

I have committed myself to the opinion that *Astrophel
and Stella* was composed, if not wholly, yet in by far
the greater part, after Lady Rich's marriage.   This
opinion being contrary to the judgment of excellent
critics, and opposed to the wishes of Sidney's admirers,
I feel bound to state my reasons.   In the first place,
then, the poems would have no meaning if they were
written for a maiden.   When a friend, quite early in
the series, objects to Sidney that

> " Desire
> Doth plunge my well-formed soul even in the mire
> Of sinful thoughts which do in ruin end,"

what significance could these words have if Stella were
still free ? Stella, throughout two-thirds of the series
(after No. xxxiii.), makes no concealment of her love
for Astrophel ; and yet she persistently repels his
ardent wooing. Why should she have done so, if she
was at liberty to obey her father's deathbed wish and
marry him ? It may here be objected that the reasons
for the breaking off of her informal engagement to
Sidney are not known ; both he and she were possibly
conscious that the marriage could not take place. To
this I answer that a wife's refusal of a lover's advances
differs from a maiden's ; and Stella's refusal in the
poems is clearly, to my mind at least, that of a married
woman. Sidney, moreover, does not hint at unkind
fate or true love hindered in its course by insurmount-
able obstacles. He has, on the other hand, plenty to
say about the unworthy husband, Stella's ignoble bondage, and Lord Rich's jealousy.

But, it has been urged, we are not sure that we
possess the sonnets and songs of *Astrophel and Stella* in
their right order. May we not conjecture that they
were either purposely or unintelligently shuffled by the
publisher, who surreptitiously obtained copies of the
loose sheets ? And again, will not close inspection of
the text reveal local and temporal allusions, by means
of which we shall be able to assign some of the more
compromising poems to dates before Penelope's
marriage ?

There are two points here for consideration, which
I will endeavour to treat separately. The first edition
of *Astrophel and Stella* was printed in 1591 by Thomas
Newman. Where this man obtained his manuscript

does not appear. But in the dedication he says : " It was my fortune not many days since to light upon the famous device of *Astrophel and Stella*, which carrying the general commendation of all men of judgment, and being reported to be one of the rarest things that ever any Englishman set abroach, I have thought good to publish it." Further on he adds : " For my part I have been very careful in the printing of it, and whereas, being spread abroad in written copies, it had gathered much corruption by ill-writers ; I have used their help and advice in correcting and restoring it to his first dignity that I know were of skill and experience in those matters." If these sentences have any meaning, it is that *Astrophel and Stella* circulated widely in manuscript, as a collected whole, and not in scattered sheets, before it fell into the hands of Newman. It was already known to the world as a " famous device," a "rare thing;" and throughout the dedication it is spoken of as a single piece. What strengthens this argument is that the Countess of Pembroke, in her lifetime, permitted *Astrophel and Stella* to be reprinted, together with her own corrected version of the *Arcadia*, without making any alteration in its arrangement.

If we examine the poems with minute attention we shall, I think, be led to the conclusion that they have not been shuffled, but that we possess them in the order in which Sidney wrote them. To begin with, the first nine sonnets form a kind of exordium. They set forth the object for which the whole series was composed, they celebrate Stella's mental and personal charms in general, they characterise Sidney's style and source of inspiration, and criticise the affectations of his

contemporaries. In the second place, we find that
many of the sonnets are written in sequence. I will
cite, for example, Nos. 31-34, Nos. 38-40, Nos. 69-72,
Nos. 87-92, Nos. 93-100. Had the order been either
unintelligently or intentionally confused, it is not probable that these sequences would have survived entire.
And upon this point I may notice that the interspersed
lyrics occur in their proper places—that is to say, in
close connection with the subject - matter of accompanying sonnets. It may thirdly be observed that
Astrophel and Stella, as we have it, exhibits a natural
rhythm and development of sentiment, from admiration and chagrin, through expectant passion, followed
by hope sustained at a high pitch of enthusiasm, down
to eventual discouragement and resignation. As Thomas
Nash said in his preface to the first edition : "The chief
actor here is Melpomene, whose dusky robes dipped in
the ink of tears as yet seem to drop when I see them
near. The argument cruel chastity, the prologue hope,
the epilogue despair." That the series ends abruptly,
as though its author had abandoned it from weariness,
should also be noticed. This is natural in the case of
lyrics, which were clearly the outpouring of the poet's
inmost feelings. When he had once determined to cast
off the yoke of a passion which could not but have been
injurious to his better self, Astrophel stopped singing.
He was not rounding off a subject artistically contemplated from outside. There was no envoy to be written
when once the aliment of love had been abandoned.

With regard to the second question I have raised,
namely, whether close inspection will not enable us to
fix dates for the composition of *Astrophel and Stella*,

and thus to rearrange the order of its pieces, I must say that very few of the poems seem to me to offer any solid ground for criticism of this kind. Sonnets 24, 35, and 37 clearly allude to Stella's married name. Sonnet 41, the famous " Having this day my horse, my hand, my lance," may refer to Sidney's assault upon the Castle of Perfect Beauty ; but since he was worsted in that mimic siege, this seems doubtful. The mention of " that sweet enemy France" might lead us equally well to assign it to the period of Anjou's visit. In either case, the date would be after Stella's betrothal to Lord Rich. Sonnet 30, "Whether the Turkish new moon minded be," points to political events in Europe which were taking place after the beginning of 1581, and consequently about the period of Penelope's marriage. These five sonnets fall within the first forty-one of a series which numbers one hundred and eight. After them I can discover nothing but allusions to facts of private life, Astrophel's absence from the Court, Stella's temporary illness, a stolen kiss, a lover's quarrel.

In conclusion, I would fain point out that any one who may have composed a series of poems upon a single theme, extending over a period of many months, will be aware how impertinent it is for an outsider to debate their order. Nothing can be more certain, in such species of composition, than that thoughts once suggested will be taken up for more elaborate handling on a future occasion. Thus the contention between love and virtue, which occurs early in *Astrophel and Stella*, is developed at length toward its close. The Platonic conception of beauty is suggested near the commencement, and is worked out in a later sequence.

Sometimes a motive from external life supplies the poet with a single lyric, which seems to interrupt the lover's monologue. Sometimes he strikes upon a vein so fruitful that it yields a succession of linked sonnets and intercalated songs.

I have attempted to explain why I regard *Astrophel and Stella* as a single whole, the arrangement of which does not materially differ from that intended by its author. I have also expressed my belief that it was written after Penelope Devereux became Lady Rich. This justifies me in saying, as I did upon a former page, that the exact date of her marriage seems to me no matter of vital importance in Sir Philip Sidney's biography. My theory of the love which it portrays, is that this was latent up to the time of her betrothal, and that the consciousness of the irrevocable at that moment made it break into the kind of regretful passion which is peculiarly suited for poetic treatment. Stella may have wasted some of Philip's time ; but it is clear that she behaved honestly, and to her lover helpfully, by the firm but gentle refusal of his overtures. Throughout these poems, though I recognise their very genuine emotion, I cannot help discerning the note of what may be described as poetical exaggeration. In other words, I do not believe that Sidney would in act have really gone so far as he professes to desire. On paper it was easy to demand more than seriously, in hot or cold blood, he would have attempted. To this artistic exaltation of a real feeling the chosen form of composition both traditionally and artistically lent itself. Finally, when all these points have been duly considered, we must not forget that society at that epoch was lenient, if not lax, in matters

of the passions. Stella's position at Court, while she
was the acknowledged mistress of Sir Charles Blount,
suffices to prove this ; nor have we any reason to suppose that Philip was, in this respect, more "a spirit
without spot" than his contemporaries. Some of his
deathbed meditations indicate sincere repentance for
past follies ; but that his liaison with Lady Rich involved nothing worse than a young man's infatuation,
appears from the pervading tone of *Astrophel and Stella.*
A motto might be chosen for it from the 66th sonnet :

> " I cannot brag of word, much less of deed."

The critical cobwebs which beset the personal romance
of *Astrophel and Stella* have now been cleared away.
Readers of these pages know how I for one interpret its
problems. Whatever opinion they may form upon a
topic which has exercised many ingenious minds, we are
able at length to approach the work of art, and to
study its beauties together. Regarding one point, I
would fain submit a word of preliminary warning. However artificial and allusive may appear the style of these
love poems, let us prepare ourselves to find real feeling
and substantial thought expressed in them. It was not
a mere rhetorical embroidery of phrases which moved
downright Ben Jonson to ask :

> " Hath not great Sidney Stella set
> Where never star shone brighter yet ?"

It was no flimsy string of pearled conceits which drew
from Richard Crashaw in his most exalted moment that
allusion to :

> " Sydnaean showers
> Of sweet discourse, whose powers
> Can crown old Winter's head with flowers."

The elder poets, into whose ken *Astrophel and Stella* swam like a thing of unimagined and unapprehended beauty, had no doubt of its sincerity. The quaintness of its tropes and the condensation of its symbolism were proofs to them of passion stirring the deep soul of a finely-gifted, highly-educated man. They read it as we read *In Memoriam*, acknowledging some obscure passages, recognising some awkwardness of incoherent utterance, but taking these on trust as evidences of the poet's heart too charged with stuff for ordinary methods of expression. What did Shakespeare make Achilles say?

> "My mind is troubled, like a fountain stirred,
> And I myself see not the bottom of it."

Charles Lamb puts this point well. "The images which lie before our feet (though by some accounted the only natural) are least natural for the high Sydnaean love to express its fancies. They may serve for the love of Tibullus, or the dear author of the *Schoolmistress;* for passions that weep and whine in elegies and pastoral ballads. I am sure Milton (and Lamb might have added Shakespeare) never loved at this rate."

The forms adopted by Sidney in his *Astrophel and Stella* sonnets are various ; but none of them correspond exactly to the Shakespearian type—three separate quatrains clinched with a final couplet. He adheres more closely to Italian models, especially in his handling of the octave ; although we find only two specimens (Nos. 29, 94) of the true Petrarchan species in the treatment of the sextet. Sidney preferred to close the stanza with a couplet. The best and most characteristic of his compositions are built in this way : two quatrains upon a

pair of rhymes, arranged as *a, b, b, a, a, b, b, a;* followed
by a quatrain *c, d, c, d,* and a couplet *e, e.* The pauses
frequently occur at the end of the eighth line, and again
at the end of the eleventh, so that the closing couplet
is not abruptly detached from the structure of the
sextet. It will be observed from the quotations which
follow that this, which I indicate as the most distinctively
Sidneyan type, is by no means invariable. To analyse
each of the many schemes under which his sonnets can
be arranged, would be unprofitable in a book which does
not pretend to deal technically with this form of stanza.
Yet I may add that he often employs a type of the
sextet, which is commoner in French than in Italian or
English poetry, with this rhyming order : *c, c, d, e, e, d.*
I have counted twenty of this sort.

The first sonnet, which is composed in lines of twelve
syllables, sets forth the argument :

" Loving in truth, and fain in verse my love to show,
    That she, dear she, might take some pleasure of my
       pain,
   Pleasure might cause her read, reading might make her
      know,
    Knowledge might pity win, and pity grace obtain ;
I sought fit words to paint the blackest face of woe,
    Studying inventions fine her wits to entertain,
Oft turning others' leaves to see if thence would flow
    Some fresh and fruitful showers upon my sun-burned
      brain.
But words came halting forth, wanting invention's stay ;
    Invention, nature's child, fled step-dame study's blows ;
Another's feet still seemed but stranger's in my way.
    Thus, great with child to speak, and helpless in my throes,
Biting my truant pen, beating myself for spite—
   ' Fool,' said my Muse to me, ' look in thy heart and
     write !' "

This means that Sidney's love was sincere ; but that he first sought expression for it in phrases studied from famous models. He wished to please his lady, and to move her pity. His efforts proved ineffectual, until the Muse came and said : "Look in thy heart and write." Like Dante, Sidney then declared himself to be one :

> " Che quando,
> Amore spira, noto ; ed a quel modo
> Ch'ei detta dentro, vo significando."
>
> *Purg.* 24. 52.

> " Love only reading unto me this art."
>
> *Astrophel and Stella*, sonnet 28.

The 3d, 6th, 15th, and 28th sonnets return to the same point. He takes poets to task, who

> " With strange similes enrich each line,
> Of herbs or beasts which Ind or Afric hold."
>
> (No. 3.)

He describes how

> " Some one his song in Jove, and Jove's strange tales attires,
> Bordered with bulls and swans, powdered with golden rain ;
> Another, humbler wit, to shepherd's pipe retires,
> Yet hiding royal blood full oft in rural vein."
>
> (No. 6.)

He inveighs against

> " You that do search for every purling spring
> Which from the ribs of old Parnassus flows ;
> And every flower, not sweet perhaps, which grows
> Near thereabouts, into your poesy wring ;
> Ye that do dictionary's method bring
> Into your rhymes, running in rattling rows ;
> You that poor Petrarch's long deceasèd woes,
> With new-born sighs, and denizened wits do sing."
>
> (No. 15.)

He girds no less against

> " You that with allegory's curious frame
> Of other's children changelings use to make."
>
> (No. 28.)

All these are on the wrong tack. Stella is sufficient source of inspiration for him, for them, for every singer. This theoretical position, does not, however, prevent him from falling into a very morass of conceits, of which we have an early example in the 9th sonnet. Marino could scarcely have executed variations more elaborate upon the single theme :

> " Queen Virtue's Court, which some call Stella's face."

I may here state that I mean to omit those passages in *Astrophel and Stella* which strike me as merely artificial. I want, if possible, to introduce readers to what is perennially and humanly valuable in the poetical record of Sir Philip Sidney's romance. More than enough will remain of emotion simply expressed, of deep thought pithily presented, to fill a longer chapter than I can dedicate to his book of the heart.

The 2d sonnet describes the growth of Sidney's passion. Love he says, neither smote him at first sight, nor aimed an upward shaft to pierce his heart on the descent.[1] Long familiarity made him appreciate Stella. Liking deepened into love. Yet at the first he neglected to make his love known. Now, too late, he finds him-

---

[1] This, at least, is how I suppose we ought to interpret the word *dribbed*. In Elizabethan English this seems to have been technically equivalent to what in archery is now called *elevating* as opposed to *shooting point blank*.

self hopelessly enslaved when the love for a married
woman can yield only torment.

> " Not at first sight, nor with a dribbèd shot,
>   Love gave the wound, which, while I breathe will
>   bleed ;
>   But known worth did in mine of time proceed,
> Till by degrees it had full conquest got.
> I saw, and liked ; I liked, but lovèd not ;
>   I loved, but straight did not what Love decreed :
>   At length to Love's decrees I forced agreed,
> Yet with repining at so partial lot.
>   Now even that footstep of lost liberty
> Is gone ; and now, like slave-born Muscovite,
>   I call it praise to suffer tyranny ;
> And now employ the remnant of my wit
>   To make myself believe that all is well,
>   While with a feeling skill I paint my hell."

In the 4th and 5th sonnets two themes are suggested,
which, later on, receive fuller development. The first is
the contention between love and virtue ; the second is
the Platonic conception of beauty as a visible image of
virtue. The latter of these motives is thus tersely set
forth in sonnet 25 :

> " The wisest scholar of the wight most wise
>   By Phoebus' doom, with sugared sentence says
> That virtue, if it once met with our eyes,
>   Strange flames of love it in our souls would raise."

Here, at the commencement of the series, Sidney
rather plays with the idea than dwells upon it :

> " True, that true beauty virtue is indeed,
>   Whereof this beauty can be but a shade,
> Which elements with mortal mixture breed.
>   True, that on earth we are but pilgrims made,
> And should in soul up to our country move ;
> True, and yet true—that I must Stella love." (No. 5.)

In the 10th sonnet he opens a dispute with Reason, which also is continued at intervals throughout the series :

> " I rather wished thee climb the Muses' hill,
>   Or reach the fruit of Nature's choicest tree,
>   Or seek heaven's course or heaven's inside to see ;
> Why should'st thou toil our thorny soil to till ?
>   Leave sense, and those which sense's objects be ;
> Deal thou with powers of thoughts, leave Love to Will."
>   (No. 10.)

The next explains how Cupid has taken possession of Stella's person ; only the fool has neglected to creep into her heart.   The 12th expands this theme, and concludes thus :

> " Thou countest Stella thine, like those whose powers
>   Having got up a breach by fighting well,
> Cry ' Victory ! this fair day all is ours ! '
>   O no ; her heart is such a citadel,
>   So fortified with wit, stored with disdain,
> That to win it is all the skill and pain."   (No. 12.)

At this point, then, of Astrophel's love-diary, Stella still held her heart inviolate, like an acropolis which falls not with the falling of the outworks.   In the 14th he replies to a friend who expostulates because he yields to the sinful desire for a married woman :

> " If that be sin which doth the manners frame,
>   Well stayed with truth in word and faith of deed,
> Ready of wit and fearing naught but shame ;
>   If that be sin which in fixed hearts doth breed
> A loathing of all loose unchastity ;
> Then love is sin, and let me sinful be."   (No. 14.)

The 16th has one fine line.   At first Sidney had trifled with love :

> " But while I thus with this young lion played,"

I fell, he says, a victim to Stella's eyes. The 18th bewails his misemployed manhood, somewhat in Shakespeare's vein :

> " My youth doth waste, my knowledge brings forth toys ;
>   My wit doth strive these passions to defend,
> Which, for reward, spoil it with vain annoys."   (No. 18.)

The 21st takes up the same theme, and combines it with that of the 14th :

> " Your words, my friend, right healthful caustics, blame
>   My young mind marred."

It is clear that Stella's love was beginning to weigh heavily upon his soul. Friends observed an alteration in him, and warned him against the indulgence of anything so ruinous as this passion for a woman who belonged to another. As yet their admonitions could be entertained and playfully put by. Sidney did not feel himself irrevocably engaged. He still trifled with love as a pleasant episode in life, a new and radiant experience. At this point two well-composed sonnets occur, which show how he behaved before the world's eyes with the burden of his nascent love upon his heart :

> " The curious wits, seeing dull pensiveness
>   Bearing itself in my long-settled eyes,
>   Whence those same fumes of melancholy rise,
> With idle pains and missing aim do guess.
> Some, that know how my spring I did address,
>   Deem that my Muse some fruit of knowledge plies ;
>   Others, because the prince of service tries,
> Think that I think state errors to redress.
> But harder judges judge ambition's rage,
>   Scourge of itself, still climbing slippery place,
> Holds my young brain captived in golden cage.

K

O fools, or over-wise ! alas, the race
Of all my thoughts hath neither stop nor start
But only Stella's eyes and Stella's heart."   (No. 23.)

" Because I oft in dark abstracted guise
        Seem most alone in greatest company,
        With dearth of words or answers quite awry
To them that would make speech of speech arise ;
They deem, and of their doom the rumour flies,
        That poison foul of bubbling pride doth lie
        So in my swelling breast, that only I
Fawn on myself and others do despise.
Yet pride, I think, doth not my soul possess,
        Which looks too oft in his unflattering glass ;
But one worse fault, ambition, I confess,
        That makes me oft my best friends overpass,
Unseen, unheard, while thought to highest place
Bends all his powers—even unto Stella's grace."
                                                (No. 27.)

Now, too, begin the series of plays upon the name
Rich, and invectives against Stella's husband. It seems
certain that Lord Rich was not worthy of his wife.
Sidney had an unbounded contempt for him. He calls
him "rich fool" and "lout," and describes Stella's bondage to him as "a foul yoke." Yet this disdain, however
rightly felt, ought not to have found vent in such
sonnets as Nos. 24 and 78. The latter degenerates into
absolute offensiveness, when, after describing the *faux
jaloux* under a transparent allegory, he winds up with
the question :

    " Is it not evil that such a devil wants horns ? "

The first section of *Astrophel and Stella* closes with
sonnet 30. Thus far Sidney has been engaged with his
poetical exordium. Thus far his love has been an

absorbing pastime rather than the business of his life.
The 31st sonnet preludes, with splendid melancholy, to
a new and deeper phase of passion :

> "With how sad steps, O moon, thou climb'st the skies !
>   How silently, and with how wan a face !
>   What, may it be that even in heavenly place
> That busy archer his sharp arrows tries ?
> Sure, if that long-with-love-acquainted eyes
>   Can judge of love, thou feel'st a lover's case ;
>   I read it in thy looks ; thy languished grace
> To me, that feel the like, thy state descries.
> Then, even of fellowship, O moon, tell me,
>   Is constant love deemed there but want of wit ?
> Are beauties there as proud as here they be ?
>   Do they above love to be loved, and yet
> Those lovers scorn whom that love doth possess ?
> Do they call virtue there ungratefulness ? "

Sidney's thoughts, throughout these poems, were
often with the night ; far oftener than Petrarch's or than
Shakespeare's. In the course of our analysis, we shall
cull many a meditation belonging to the hours before the
dawn, and many a pregnant piece of midnight imagery.
What can be more quaintly accurate in its condensed
metaphors than the following personification of dreams ?

> "Morpheus, the lively son of deadly sleep,
>   Witness of life to them that living die,
>   A prophet oft, and oft an history,
> A poet eke, as humours fly or creep."   (No. 32.)

In the 33d sonnet we find the first hint that Stella
might have reciprocated Astrophel's love :

> "I might, unhappy word, woe me, I might !
>   And then would not, or could not, see my bliss:

> Till now, wrapped in a most infernal night,
> 　I find how heavenly day, wretch, I did miss.
> Heart, rend thyself ; thou dost thyself but right !
> 　No lovely Paris made thy Helen his ;
> No force, no fraud robbed thee of thy delight,
> 　Nor fortune of thy fortune author is !
> But to myself myself did give the blow,
> 　While too much wit, forsooth, so troubled me,
> That I respects for both our sakes must show :
> 　And yet could not, by rising morn foresee
> How fair a day was near : O punished eyes,
> That I had been more foolish or more wise !" (No. **33**.)

This sonnet has generally been taken to refer to Sidney's indolence before the period of Stella's marriage ; in which case it expands the line of No. 2 :

> " I loved, but straight did not what Love decrees."

It may, however, have been written upon the occasion of some favourable chance which he neglected to seize ; and the master phrase of the whole composition "respects for both our sakes," rather points to this interpretation. We do not know enough of the obstacles to Sidney's match with Penelope Devereux to be quite sure whether such "respects" existed while she was at liberty.

There is nothing now left for him but to vent his regrets and vain longings in words. But what are empty words, what consolation can they bring?

> " And, ah, what hope that hope should once see day,
> 　Where Cupid is sworn page to chastity ?"　　(No. **35**.)

Each day Stella makes new inroads upon the fortress of his soul.

> " Through my long-battered eyes
> Whole armies of thy beauties entered in :
> And there long since, love, thy lieutenant lies."
>
> (No. 36.)

Stella can weep over tales of unhappy lovers she has never known. Perhaps if she could think his case a fable, she might learn to pity him :

> " Then think, my dear, that you in me do read
> Of lover's ruin some thrice-sad tragedy.
> I am not I ; pity the tale of me !"   (No. 45.)

He entreats her not to shun his presence or withdraw the heaven's light of her eyes :

> " Soul's joy, bend not those morning stars from me,
> Where virtue is made strong by beauty's might ! "

Nay, let her gaze upon him, though that splendour should wither up his life :

> " A kind of grace it is to kill with speed."   (No. 48.)

He prays to her, as to a deity raised high above the stress and tempest of his vigilant desires :

> " Alas, if from the height of virtue's throne
> Thou canst vouchsafe the influence of a thought
> Upon a wretch that long thy grace hath sought,
> Weigh then how I by thee am overthrown ! "   (No. 40.)

It is here, too, that the pathetic outcry, " my mind, now of the basest," now (that is) of the lowest and most humbled, is forced from him. Then, returning to the theme of Stella's unconquerable virtue, he calls her eyes

> " The schools where Venus hath learned chastity."
>
> (No. 42.)

From the midst of this group shine forth, like stars, two
sonnets of pure but of very different lustre :

> " Come, sleep ! O sleep, the certain knot of peace,
>   The baiting-place of wit, the balm of woe,
> The poor man's wealth, the prisoner's release,
>   Th' indifferent judge between the high and low !
> With shield of proof shield me from out the press
>   Of those fierce darts despair at me doth throw ;
> O make in me those civil wars to cease ;
>   I will good tribute pay, if thou do so.
> Take thou of me smooth pillows, sweetest bed,
>   A chamber deaf of noise and blind of light,
> A rosy garland and a weary head ;
>   And if these things, as being thine in right,
> Move not thy heavy grace, thou shalt in me,
> Livelier than elsewhere, Stella's image see."   (No. 39.)

> " Having this day my horse, my hand, my lance
>   Guided so well that I obtained the prize,
>   Both by the judgment of the English eyes
> And of some sent from that sweet enemy France ;
> Horsemen my skill in horsemanship advance,
>   Town-folks my strength ; a daintier judge applies
>   His praise to sleight which from good use doth rise ;
> Some lucky wits impute it but to chance ;
> Others, because of both sides I do take
>   My blood from them who did excel in this,
> Think nature me a man-at-arms did make.
>   How far they shot awry ! the true cause is,
> Stella looked on, and from her heavenly face
> Sent forth the beams which made so fair my race."
>   (No. 41.)

Sometimes he feels convinced that this passion will be
his ruin, and strives, but strives in vain as yet, against it :

> " Virtue, awake !   Beauty but beauty is ;
>   I may, I must, I can, I will, I do
> Leave following that which it is gain to miss.
>   Let her go !   Soft, but here she comes !   Go to,

Unkind, I love you not!   O me, that eye
Doth make my heart to give my tongue the lie!"

(No. 47.)

Sometimes he draws strength from the same passion; at another time the sight of Stella well-nigh unnerves his trained bridle-hand, and suspends his lance in rest. This from the tilting-ground is worth preserving:

" In martial sports I had my cunning tried,
    And yet to break more staves did me address,
    While with the people's shouts, I must confess,
Youth, luck, and praise even filled my veins with pride;
When Cupid, having me, his slave, descried
    In Mars's livery prancing in the press,
    'What now, Sir Fool!' said he : I would no less :
'Look here, I say!' I looked, and Stella spied,
Who hard by made a window send forth light.
    My heart then quaked, then dazzled were mine eyes;
One hand forgot to rule, th' other to fight,
    Nor trumpet's sound I heard nor friendly cries :
My foe came on, and beat the air for me,
Till that her blush taught me my shame to see."

(No. 53.)

The quaint author of the *Life and Death of Sir Philip Sidney*, prefixed to the *Arcadia*, relates how — "many nobles of the female sex, venturing as far as modesty would permit, to signify their affections unto him; Sir Philip will not read the characters of their love, though obvious to every eye." This passage finds illustration in the next sonnet:

"Because I breathe not love to every one,
    Nor do not use set colours for to wear,
    Nor nourish special locks of vowèd hair,
Nor give each speech a full point of a groan ;
    The courtly nymphs, acquainted with the moan

Of them which in their lips love's standard bear,
  'What he!' say they of me: 'now I dare swear
He cannot love; no, no, let him alone!'
And think so still, so Stella know my mind!
  Profess indeed I do not Cupid's art:
But you, fair maids, at length this true shall find,
  That his right badge is but worn in the heart:
Dumb swans, not chattering pies, do lovers prove;
They love indeed who quake to say they love."

(No. 54.)

Up to this point Stella has been Sidney's saint, the
adored object, remote as a star from his heart's sphere.
Now at last she confesses that she loves him. But her
love is of pure and sisterly temper; and she mingles its
avowal with noble counsels, little to his inclination.

"Late tired with woe, even ready for to pine
  With rage of love, I called my love unkind;
She in whose eyes love, though unfelt, doth shine,
  Sweet said that I true love in her should find.
I joyed; but straight thus watered was my wine:
  That love she did, but loved a love not blind;
Which would not let me, whom she loved, decline
  From nobler course, fit for my birth and mind;
And therefore by her love's authority
Willed me these tempests of vain love to fly,
  And anchor fast myself on virtue's shore.
Alas, if this the only metal be
Of love new-coined to help my beggary,
  Dear, love me not, that you may love me more!"

(No. 62.)

His heated senses rebel against her admonitions:

" No more, my dear, no more these counsels try;
  O give my passions leave to run their race;
  Let fortune lay on me her worst disgrace;
  Let folk o'ercharged with brain against me cry;

> Let clouds bedim my face, break in mine eye;
>   Let me no steps but of lost labour trace;
>   Let all the earth with scorn recount my case;
> But do not will me from my love to fly!"   (No. 64.)

Then he seeks relief in trifles. Playing upon his own coat of arms ("or, a pheon azure"), he tells Love how he nursed him in his bosom, and how they both must surely be of the same lineage:

> "For when, naked boy, thou couldst no harbour find
>   In this old world, grown now so too-too wise,
> I lodged thee in my heart, and being blind
>   By nature born, I gave to thee mine eyes . . .
> Yet let this thought thy tigrish courage pass,
>   That I perhaps am somewhat kin to thee;
> Since in thine arms, if learned fame truth hath spread,
> Thou bear'st the arrow, I the arrow head."   (No. 65.)

Stella continues to repress his ardour:

> "I cannot brag of word, much less of deed . . .
>   Desire still on stilts of fear doth go."   (No. 66.)

Yet once she blushed when their eyes met; and her blush "guilty seemed of love." Therefore he expostulates with her upon her cruelty:

> "Stella, the only planet of my light,
>   Light of my life, and life of my desire,
>   Chief good whereto my hope doth only aspire,
> World of my wealth, and heaven of my delight;
> Why dost thou spend the treasures of thy sprite,
>   With voice more fit to wed Amphion's lyre,
>   Seeking to quench in me the noble fire
> Fed by thy worth and kindled by thy sight?"
>
>   (No. 68.)

Suddenly, to close this contention, we find him at the height of his felicity. Stella has relented, yielding him

the kingdom of her heart, but adding the condition that
he must love, as she does, virtuously :

> "O joy too high for my low style to show!
>   O bliss fit for a nobler state than me !
>   Envy, put out thine eyes, lest thou do see
> What oceans of delight in me do flow!
> My friend, that oft saw through all masks my woe,
>   Come, come, and let me pour myself on thee:
>   Gone is the winter of my misery ;
> My spring appears ; O see what here doth grow !
> For Stella hath, with words where faith doth shine,
>   Of her high heart given me the monarchy ;
> I, I, O I, may say that she is mine !
>   And though she give but thus conditionally,
> This realm of bliss, while virtuous course I take,
> No kings be crowned but they some covenants make."
>   (No. 69.)

Now, the stanzas which have so long eased his sadness,
shall be turned to joy :

> " Sonnets be not bound prentice to annoy ;
>   Trebles sing high, so well as basses deep ;
>   Grief but Love's winter-livery is ; the boy
>   Hath cheeks to smile, so well as eyes to weep."

And yet, with the same breath, he says :

> " Wise silence is best music unto bliss."   (No. 70.)

In the next sonnet he shows that Stella's virtuous conditions do not satisfy.   True it is that whoso looks upon
her face,

> " There shall he find all vices' overthrow,
>   Not by rude force, but sweetest sovereignty
> Of reason.   .   .   .   .
>   But, ah, desire still cries : Give me some food !"
>   (No. 71.)

Farewell then to desire :

> " Desire, though thou my old companion art,
>   And oft so clings to my pure love that I
>   One from the other scarcely can descry,
>   While each doth blow the fire of my heart ;
>   Now from thy fellowship I needs must part."
>
> (No. 72.)

It is characteristic of the fluctations both of feeling
and circumstance, so minutely followed in Astrophel's
love-diary, that, just at this moment, when he has resolved to part with desire, he breaks out into this
jubilant song upon the stolen kiss :

> " Have I caught my heavenly jewel,
>   Teaching sleep most fair to be !
>   Now will I teach her that she,
>   When she wakes, is too-too cruel.

> " Since sweet sleep her eyes hath charmèd,
>   The two only darts of Love,
>   Now will I with that boy prove
>   Some play while he is disarmèd.

> " Her tongue, waking, still refuseth,
>   Giving frankly niggard no :
>   Now will I attempt to know
>   What no her tongue, sleeping, useth.

> " See the hand that, waking, guardeth,
>   Sleeping, grants a free resort :
>   Now will I invade the fort ;
>   Cowards Love with loss rewardeth.

> " But, O fool, think of the danger
>   Of her high and just disdain !
>   Now will I, alas, refrain :
>   Love fears nothing else but anger.

" Yet those lips, so sweetly swelling,
    Do invite a stealing kiss :
    Now will I but venture this ;
Who will read, must first learn spelling.

" Oh, sweet kiss ! but ah, she's waking ;
    Lowering beauty chastens me :
    Now will I for fear hence flee ;
Fool, more fool, for no mere taking !"

Several pages are occupied with meditations on this
lucky kiss.   The poet's thoughts turn to alternate
ecstasy and wantonness.

" I never drank of Aganippe's well,
    Nor ever did in shade of Tempe sit,
And Muses scorn with vulgar brains to dwell ;
    Poor layman I, for sacred rites unfit !
        .   .   .   .
" How falls it then that with so smooth an ease
    My thoughts I speak ; and what I speak doth flow
In verse, and that my verse test wits doth please ?"

The answer of course is :

" Thy lips are sweet, inspired with Stella's kiss."
                                            (No. 74.)

In this mood we find him praising Edward IV., who
risked his kingdom for Lady Elizabeth Grey.

" Of all the kings that ever here did reign,
    Edward, named fourth, as first in praise I name ;
Not for his fair outside, nor well-lined brain,
    Although less gifts imp feathers oft on fame :
Nor that he could, young-wise, wise-valiant, frame
    His sire's revenge, joined with a kingdom's gain ;
And gained by Mars, could yet mad Mars so tame
    That balance weighed what sword did late obtain :

Nor that he made the flower-de-luce so 'fraid,
  Though strongly hedged of bloody lions' paws,
That witty Lewis to him a tribute paid :
  Not this, not that, nor any such small cause ;
But only for this worthy knight durst prove
  To lose his crown rather than fail his love."

(No. 75.)

A sonnet on the open road, in a vein of conceits worthy
of Philostratus, closes the group inspired by Stella's
kiss :

" High way, since you my chief Parnassus be,
  And that my Muse, to some ears not unsweet,
  Tempers her words to trampling horse's feet
More oft than to a chamber-melody :
Now blessèd you bear onward blessèd me
  To her, where I my heart, safe-left shall meet,
  My Muse and I must you of duty greet
With thanks and wishes, wishing thankfully.
Be you still fair, honoured by public heed ;
  By no encroachment wronged, nor time forgot ;
Nor blamed for blood, nor shamed for sinful deed ;
  And that you know I envy you no lot
Of highest wish, I wish you so much bliss—
Hundreds of years you Stella's feet may kiss."

(No. 84.)

And now a change comes over the spirit of Sidney's
dream. It is introduced, as the episode of the stolen
kiss was, by a song. We do not know on what occasion he may have found himself alone with Stella at
night, when her husband's jealousy was sleeping, the
house closed, and her mother in bed. But the lyric
refers, I think, clearly to some real incident—perhaps
at Leicester House :

" Only joy, now here you are
  Fit to hear and ease my care,

Let my whispering voice obtain
Sweet reward for sharpest pain ;
Take me to thee and thee to me :—
' No, no, no, no, my dear, let be !'

" Night hath closed all in her cloak,
Twinkling stars love-thoughts provoke ;
Danger hence, good care doth keep ;
Jealousy himself doth sleep ;
Take me to thee and thee to me :—
' No, no, no, no, my dear, let be !'

" Better place no wit can find
Cupid's knot to loose or bind ;
These sweet flowers, our fine bed, too
Us in their best language woo :
Take me to thee and thee to me :—
' No, no, no, no, my dear, let be !'

" This small light the moon bestows,
Serves thy beams but to disclose ;
So to raise my hap more high,
Fear not else ; none can us spy :
Take me to thee and thee to me :—
' No, no, no, no, my dear, let be !'

" That you heard was but a mouse ;
Dumb sleep holdeth all the house ;
Yet asleep, methinks they say,
Young fools, take time while you may :
Take me to thee and thee to me :—
' No, no, no, no, my dear, let be !'

" Niggard time threats, if we miss
This large offer of our bliss,
Long stay ere he grant the same :
Sweet then, while each thing doth frame,
Take me to thee and thee to me :—
' No, no, no, no, my dear, let be !'

" Your fair mother is a-bed,
    Candles out and curtains spread ;
    She thinks you do letters write:
    Write, but first let me endite :
    Take me to thee and thee to me :—
    ' No, no, no, no, my dear, let be !'

" Sweet, alas ! why strive you thus ?
    Concord better fitteth us ;
    Leave to Mars the strife of hands ;
    Your power in your beauty stands :
    Take me to thee and thee to me :—
    ' No, no, no, no, my dear, let be !'

" Woe to me ! and do you swear
    Me to hate ? but I forbear :
    Cursèd be my destinies all,
    That brought me so high to fall !
    Soon with my death I'll please thee :—
    ' No, no, no, no, my dear, let be !'"

It will be noticed that to all his pleadings, passionate
or playful, and (it must be admitted) of very questionable morality, she returns a steadfast No ! This accounts
for the altered tone of the next sonnet. In the 85th he
had indulged golden, triumphant visions, and had bade
his heart be moderate in the fruition of its bliss. Now
he exclaims :

" Alas ! whence came this change of looks ?   If I
    Have changed desert, let mine own conscience be
    A still-felt plague to self-condemning me ;
Let woe gripe on my heart, shame load mine eye !"
                                        (No. 86.)

He has pressed his suit too far, and Stella begins to
draw back from their common danger. Five songs fol-

low in quick succession, one of which prepares us for the
denouement of the love-drama :

> " In a grove most rich of shade,
> Where birds wanton music made,
> May, then young, his pied weeds showing,
> New-perfumed with flowers fresh growing :

> " Astrophel with Stella sweet
> Did for mutual comfort meet ;
> Both within themselves oppressèd,
> But each in the other blessèd.

> " Him great harms had taught much care,
> Her fair neck a foul yoke bare ;
> But her sight his cares did banish,
> In his sight her yoke did vanish.

> " Wept they had, alas, the while ;
> But now tears themselves did smile,
> While their eyes, by Love directed,
> Interchangeably reflected."

For a time the lovers sat thus in silence, sighing and
gazing, until Love himself broke out into a passionate
apostrophe from the lips of Astrophel :

> " Grant, O grant ! but speech, alas,
> Fails me, fearing on to pass :
> Grant, O me ! what am I saying ?
> But no fault there is in praying.

> " Grant, O dear, on knees I pray
> (Knees on ground he then did stay)
> That not I, but since I love you,
> Time and place for me may move you.

> " Never season was more fit ;
> Never room more apt for it ;
> Smiling air allows my reason ;
> These birds sing, ' Now use the season.'

"This small wind, which so sweet is,
   See how it the leaves doth kiss ;
   Each tree in his best attiring,
   Sense of love to love inspiring.

" Love makes earth the water drink,
   Love to earth makes water sink ;
   And if dumb things be so witty,
   Shall a heavenly grace want pity ?"

To this and to yet more urgent wooing Stella replies
in stanzas which are sweetly dignified, breathing the
love she felt, but dutifully repressed.

" Astrophel, said she, my love,
   Cease in these effects to prove ;
   Now be still, yet still believe me,
   Thy grief more than death would grieve me.

" If that any thought in me
   Can taste comfort but of thee,
   Let me, fed with hellish anguish,
   Joyless, hopeless, endless languish.

" If those eyes you praisèd be
   Half so dear as you to me,
   Let me home return stark blinded
   Of those eyes, and blinder minded ;

" If to secret of my heart
   I do any wish impart
   Where thou art not foremost placèd,
   Be both wish and I defacèd.

" If more may be said, I say
   All my bliss in thee I lay ;
   If thou love, my love, content thee,
   For all love, all faith is meant thee.

" Trust me, while I thee deny,
  In myself the smart I try ;
  Tyrant honour doth thus use thee,
  Stella's self might not refuse thee.

" Therefore, dear, this no more move,
  Lest, though I not leave thy love,
  Which too deep in me is framèd,
  I should blush when thou art namèd.

" Therewithal away she went,
  Leaving him to [so ?] passion rent
  With what she had done and spoken,
  That therewith my song is broken."

The next song records Astrophel's hard necessity of
parting from Stella. But why—

" Why, alas, doth she thus swear
  That she loveth me so dearly ?"

The group of sonnets which these lyrics introduce
lead up to the final rupture, not indeed of heart and
will, but of imposed necessity, which separates the
lovers. Stella throughout plays a part which compels
our admiration, and Astrophel brings himself at length
to obedience. The situation has become unbearable to
her. She loves, and, what is more, she has confessed
her love. But, at any price, for her own sake, for his
sake, for honour, for duty, for love itself, she must free
them both from the enchantment which is closing round
them. Therefore the path which hitherto has been
ascending through fair meadows to the height of rapture,
now descends upon the other side. It is for Sidney a
long road of sighs and tears, rebellions and heart-aches,
a veritable *via dolorosa*, ending, however, in conquest over

self and tranquillity of conscience. For, as he sang in happier moments :

> " For who indeed infelt affection bears,
>> So captives to his saint both soul and sense,
> That, wholly hers, all selfness he forbears ;
>> Then his desires he learns, his life's course thence."
>>>> (No. 61.)

In the hour of their parting Stella betrays her own emotion :

> " Alas, I found that she with me did smart ;
>> I saw that tears did in her eyes appear."
>>>> (No. 87.)

After this follow five pieces written in absence :

> " Tush, absence ! while thy mists eclipse that light,
> My orphan sense flies to the inward sight,
> Where memory sets forth the beams of love."
>>>> (No. 88.)

> " Each day seems long, and longs for long-stayed night ;
>> The night, as tedious, woos the approach of day :
> Tired with the dusty toils of busy day,
> Languished with horrors of the silent night,
> Suffering the evils both of day and night,
>> While no night is more dark than is my day,
> Nor no day hath less quiet than my night."
>>>> (No. 89.)

He gazes on other beauties ; amber-coloured hair, milk-white hands, rosy cheeks, lips sweeter and redder than the rose :

> " They please, I do confess, they please mine eyes ;
>> But why ? because of you they models be,
> Models, such be wood-globes of glistering skies."
>>>> (No. 91.)

A friend speaks to him of Stella :

" You say, forsooth, you left her well of late ;—
    O God, think you *that* satisfies my care ?
I would know whether she did sit or walk ;
    How clothed, how waited on ; sighed she, or smiled ;
Whereof, with whom, how often did she talk ;
    With what pastimes Time's journey she beguiled ;
If her lips deigned to sweeten my poor name.—
Say all ; and all well said, still say the same."

(No. 92.)

Interpolated in this group is a more than usually fluent sonnet, in which Sidney disclaims all right to call himself a poet :

"Stella, think not that I by verse seek fame,
    Who seek, who hope, who love, who live but thee ;
    Thine eyes my pride, thy lips my history :
If thou praise not, all other praise is shame.
Nor so ambitious am I as to frame
    A nest for my young praise in laurel-tree ;
    In truth I swear I wish not there should be
Graved in my epitaph a poet's name.
Nor, if I would, could I just title make
    That any laud thereof to me should grow,
Without my plumes from other wings I take ;
    For nothing from my wit or will doth flow,
Since all my words thy beauty doth endite,
And love doth hold my hand and makes me write."

(No. 90.)

The sonnets in absence are closed by a song, which, as usual, introduces a new motive. It begins "O dear life," and indulges a far too audacious retrospect over the past happiness of a lover. If, as seems possible from an allusion in No. 84, he was indiscreet enough to communicate his poems to friends, this lyric may have roused the jealousy of Stella's husband and exposed her to hard treatment or reproaches.   At any rate, something he had said or done caused her pain, and he breaks out into incoherent self-revilings :

> "O fate, O fault, O curse, child of my bliss ! . . .
>   Through me, wretch me, even Stella vexèd is . . .
>   I have (live I, and know this ?) harmèd thee . . .
>   I cry thy sighs, my dear, thy tears I bleed."
>
> (No. 93.)

Should any one doubt the sincerity of accent here, let him peruse the next seven sonnets, which are written in sequence upon the same theme.

> " Grief, find the words ; for thou hast made my brain
>   So dark with misty vapours which arise
>   From out thy heavy mould, that inbent eyes
>   Can scarce discern the shape of mine own pain."
>
> (No. 94.)

> " Yet sighs, dear sighs, indeed true friends you are,
>   That do not leave your left friend at the worst ;
>   But, as you with my breast I oft have nursed,
>   So, grateful now, you wait upon my care.
>
>   .   .   .   .   .
>
>   " Nay, Sorrow comes with such main rage that he
>   Kills his own children, tears, finding that they
>   By Love were made apt to consort with me:
>   Only, true sighs, you do not go away."   (No. 95.)

The night is heavier, more irksome to him ; and yet he finds in it the parallel of his own case :

> " Poor Night in love with Phœbus' light,
>   And endlessly despairing of his grace."   (No. 97.)

The bed becomes a place of torment :

> " While the black horrors of the silent night
>   Paint woe's black face so lively to my sight,
>   That tedious leisure marks each wrinkled line."
>
> (No. 98.)

Only at dawn can he find ease in slumber. The sonnet, in which this motive is developed, illustrates Sidney's method of veiling definite and simple thoughts in abstruse and yet exact phrases. We feel impelled to say that there is something Shakespearean in the style. But we must remember that Shakespeare's sonnets were at this time locked up within his brain, as the flower is in the bud.

> " When far-spent night persuades each mortal eye
>   To whom nor art nor nature granteth light,
>   To lay his then mark-wanting shafts of sight
>   Closed with their quivers in sleep's armoury ;
>   With windows ope then most my mind doth lie
>   Viewing the shape of darkness, and delight
>   Takes in that sad hue, which with the inward night
>   Of his mazed powers keeps perfect harmony :
>   But when birds charm, and that sweet air which is
>   Morn's messenger with rose-enamelled skies
>   Calls each wight to salute the flower of bliss ;
>   In tomb of lids then buried are mine eyes,
>   Forced by their lord who is ashamed to find
>   Such light in sense with such a darkened mind."
>
> (No. 99.)

Two sonnets upon Stella's illness (to which I should be inclined to add the four upon this topic printed in Constable's *Diana*) may be omitted. But I cannot refrain from quoting the last song. It is in the form of a dialogue at night beneath Stella's window. Though apparently together at the Court, he had received express commands from her to abstain from her society; the reason of which can perhaps be found in No. 104. This sonnet shows that " envious wits " were commenting upon their intimacy; and Sidney had compromised her by wearing stars upon his armour. Anyhow he is now reduced to roaming the streets in darkness, hoping to obtain a glimpse of his beloved.

> " ' Who is it that this dark night
> Underneath my window plaineth ?'
> It is one who from thy sight
> Being, ah, exiled disdaineth
> Every other vulgar light.

> " ' Why, alas, and are you he?
> Be not yet those fancies changèd ?'
> Dear, when you find change in me,
> Though from me you be estrangèd,
> Let my change to ruin be.

> " ' Well, in absence this will die ;
> Leave to see, and leave to wonder.'
> Absence sure will help, if I
> Can learn how myself to sunder
> From what in my heart doth lie.

> " ' But time will these thoughts remove ;
> Time doth work what no man knoweth.'
> Time doth as the subject prove ;
> With time still the affection groweth
> In the faithful turtle-dove.

> " ' What if ye new beauties see ;
> Will not they stir new affection ?'
> I will think they pictures be ;
> Image-like of saints' perfection,
> Poorly counterfeiting thee.

" ' But your reason's purest light
   Bids you leave such minds to nourish.'
Dear, do reason no such spite !
   Never doth thy beauty flourish
   More than in my reason's sight.

" ' But the wrongs Love bears will make
   Love at length leave undertaking.'
No ! the more fools it doth shake,
   In a ground of so firm making
   Deeper still they drive the stake.

" ' Peace, I think that some give ear ;
   Come no more lest I get anger !'
Bliss, I will my bliss forbear,
   Fearing, sweet, you to endanger ;
   But my soul shall harbour there.

" ' Well, begone ; begone, I say ;
   Lest that Argus' eyes perceive you !'
O unjust is fortune's sway,
   Which can make me thus to leave you ;
   And from louts to run away !"

A characteristic but rather enigmatical sonnet follows
this lyric. It is another night scene. Sidney, watching
from his window, just misses the sight of Stella as her
carriage hurries by :

" Cursed be the page from whom the bad torch fell ;
   Cursed be the night which did your strife resist ;
   Cursed be the coachman that did drive so fast."

(No. 105.)

Then *Astrophel and Stella* closes abruptly, with those
disconnected sonnets, in one of which the word "despair"
occurring justifies Nash's definition of " the epilogue,
Despair " :

" But soon as thought of thee breeds my delight,
    And my young soul flutters to thee his nest,
    Most rude Despair, my daily unbidden guest,
Clips straight my wings, straight wraps me in his night."
                                                (No. 108.)

Stella's prudent withdrawal of herself from Sidney's
company begins to work with salutary effect upon his
passion. As that cools or fades for want of nourishment,
so the impulse to write declines ; and the poet's sincerity
is nowhere better shown than in the sudden and ragged
ending of his work. I doubt whether the two sonnets
on Desire and Love, which Dr. Grosart has transferred
from the Miscellaneous Poems and printed here as Nos.
109 and 110, were really meant to form part of *Astrophel
and Stella.* They strike me as retrospective, composed
in a mood of stern and somewhat bitter meditation on
the past, and probably after some considerable interval ;
yet the Latin epigraph attached to the second has the
force of an envoy. Moreover, they undoubtedly represent the attitude of mind in which Sidney bade farewell
to unhallowed love, and which enabled him loyally to
plight his troth to Frances Walsingham. Therefore it
will not be inappropriate to close the analysis of his love
poetry upon this note. No one, reading them, will fail
to be struck with their resemblance to Shakespeare's
superb sonnets upon Lust and Death (" The expense of
spirit" and " Poor soul, thou centre "), which are perhaps the two most completely powerful sonnets in our
literature :

" Thou blind man's mark, thou fool's self-chosen snare,
    Fond fancy's scum, and dregs of scattered thought ;
    Band of all evils ; cradle of causeless care ;
    Thou web of will whose end is never wrought !

Desire, desire !   I have too dearly bought
    With price of mangled mind thy worthless ware ;
Too long, too long, asleep thou hast me brought,
    Who shouldst my mind to higher things prepare.
But yet in vain thou hast my ruin sought ;
    In vain thou mad'st me to vain things aspire ;
    In vain thou kindlest all thy smoky fire :
For virtue hath this better lesson taught—
    Within myself to seek my only hire,
    Desiring naught but how to kill desire.

" Leave me, O Love, which reachest but to dust ;
    And thou, my mind, aspire to higher things ;
Grow rich in that which never taketh rust ;
    Whatever fades, but fading pleasure brings.
Draw in thy beams, and humble all thy might
    To that sweet yoke where lasting freedoms be,
Which breaks the clouds and opens forth the light,
    That doth but shine and give us sight to see.
O take fast hold ; let that light be thy guide
    In this small course which birth draws out to death ;
And think how evil becometh him to slide,
    Who seeketh heaven and comes of heavenly breath.
Then farewell, world ! thy uttermost I see :
Eternal Love, maintain thy life in me ! "

"Splendidis Longum Valedico Nugis."

CHAPTER VII

"THE DEFENCE OF POESY"

FULKE GREVILLE, touching upon the *Arcadia*, says that Sidney " purposed no monuments of books to the world." " If his purpose had been to leave his memory in books, I am confident, in the right use of logic, philosophy, history, and poesy, nay even in the most ingenious of mechanical arts, he would have showed such tracts of a searching and judicious spirit as the professors of every faculty would have striven no less for him than the seven cities did to have Homer of their sept. But the truth is : his end was not writing, even while he wrote ; nor his knowledge moulded for tables or schools ; but both his wit and understanding bent upon his heart, to make himself and others, not in words or opinion, but in life and action, good and great."

"His end was not writing, even while he wrote." This is certain ; the whole tenor of Sidney's career proves his determination to subordinate self-culture of every kind to the ruling purpose of useful public action. It will also be remembered that none of his compositions were printed during his lifetime or with his sanction. Yet he had received gifts from nature which placed him, as a critic, high above the average of his contem-

poraries. He was no mean poet when he sang as
love dictated. He had acquired and assimilated various
stores of knowledge. He possessed an exquisite and
original taste, a notable faculty for the marshalling of
arguments, and a persuasive eloquence in exposition.
These qualities inevitably found their exercise in writing ;
and of all Sidney's writings the one with which we have
to deal now, is the ripest.

Judging by the style alone, I should be inclined to
place *The Defence of Poesy* among his later works. But we
have no certain grounds for fixing the year of its composition. Probably the commonly accepted date of 1581
is the right one. In the year 1579 Stephen Gosson
dedicated to Sidney, without asking his permission, an
invective against "poets, pipers, players, and their ex-
cusers," which he called *The School of Abuse*. Spenser
observes that Gosson "was for his labour scorned ; if at
least it lie in the goodness of that nature to scorn. Such
folly is it not to regard aforehand the nature and quality
of him to whom we dedicate our books." It is possible
therefore that *The School of Abuse* and other treatises
emanating from Puritan hostility to culture, suggested
this Apology. Sidney rated poetry highest among the
functions of the human intellect. His name had been
used to give authority and currency to a clever attack
upon poets. He felt the weight of argument to be
on his side, and was conscious of his ability to conduct
the cause. With what serenity of spirit, sweetness of
temper, humour, and easy strength of style—at one time
soaring to enthusiasm, at another playing with his subject,—he performed the task, can only be appreciated
by a close perusal of the essay. It is indeed the model

for such kinds of composition—a work which combines the quaintness and the blitheness of Elizabethan literature with the urbanity and reserve of a later period.

Sidney begins by numbering himself among "the paper-blurrers," " who, I know not by what mischance, in these my not old years and idlest times, having slipped into the title of a poet, am provoked to say something unto you in the defence of that my unelected vocation." Hence it is his duty " to make a pitiful defence of poor poetry, which from almost the highest estimation of learning, is fallen to be the laughing-stock of children." Underlying Sidney's main argument we find the proposition that to attack poetry is the same as attacking culture in general ; therefore, at the outset, he appeals to all professors of learning : will they inveigh against the mother of arts and sciences, the "first nurse, whose milk by little and little enabled them to feed afterwards of tougher knowledge?" Musæus, Homer, and Hesiod lead the solemn pomp of the Greek writers. Dante, Petrarch, and Boccaccio in Italy, Gower and Chaucer in England came before prose-authors. The earliest philosophers, Empedocles and Parmenides, Solon and Tyrtæus, committed their metaphysical speculations, their gnomic wisdom, their martial exhortation, to verse. And even Plato, if rightly considered, was a poet: "in the body of his work, though the inside and strength were philosophy, the skin as it were, and beauty, depended most of poetry." Herodotus called his books by the names of the Muses : " both he and all the rest that followed him, either stole or usurped of poetry their passionate describing of passions, the many particularities of battles

which no man could affirm." They also put imaginary
speeches into the mouths of kings and captains. The
very names which the Greeks and Romans, "the authors
of most of our sciences," gave to poets, show the estimation in which they held them. The Romans called the
poet *vates*, or prophet; the Greeks ποιητής, or maker, a
word, by the way, which coincides with English custom.
What can be higher in the scale of human understanding than this faculty of *making*?   Sidney enlarges upon
its significance, following a line of thought which Tasso
summed up in one memorable sentence: "There is no
Creator but God and the Poet."

He now advances a definition, which is substantially
the same as Aristotle's: "Poesy is an art of imitation;
that is to say, a representing, counterfeiting, or figuring
forth: to speak metaphorically, a speaking picture; with
this end to teach and delight."   Of poets there have been
three general kinds: first, "they that did imitate the in-
conceivable excellences of God;" secondly, "they that
deal with matter philosophical, either moral or natural
or astronomical or historical;" thirdly, "right poets . . .
which most properly do imitate, to teach and delight;
and to imitate, borrow nothing of what is, hath been, or
shall be; but range only, reined with learned discretion,
into the divine consideration of what may be and should
be."   The preference given to the third kind of poets
may be thus explained: The first group are limited to
setting forth fixed theological conceptions; the second
have their material supplied them by the sciences; but
the third are the makers and creators of ideals for warning and example.

Poets may also be classified according to the several

species of verse. But this implies a formal and mislead-
ing limitation. Sidney, like Milton and like Shelley,
will not have poetry confined to metre: "apparelled
verse being but an ornament, and no cause to poetry;
since there have been many most excellent poets that
have never versified, and now swarm many versifiers that
need never answer to the name of poets." Xenophon's
"Cyropædia," the "Theagenes and Chariclea" of Helio-
dorus, are cited as true poems; "and yet both these wrote
in prose." "It is not rhyming and versing that maketh a
poet; but it is that feigning notable images of virtues, vices,
or what else, with that delightful teaching, which must
be the right describing note to know a poet by." Truly
"the senate of poets have chosen verse as their fittest
raiment;" but this they did, because they meant, "as in
matter they passed all in all, so in manner to go beyond
them." "Speech, next to reason, is the greatest gift bestowed upon mortality;" and verse "which most doth
polish that blessing of speech," is, therefore, the highest
investiture of poetic thought.

Having thus defined his conception of poetry, Sidney
inquires into the purpose of all learning. "This purify-
ing of wit, this enriching of memory, enabling of judgment, and enlarging of conceit, which commonly we call
learning, under what name soever it come forth, or to
what immediate end soever it be directed; the final end
is to lead and draw us to as high a perfection as our
degenerate souls, made worse by their clay lodgings,
can be capable of." All the branches of learning subserve
the royal or architectonic science, "which stands, as I
think, in the knowledge of a man's self in the ethic and
politic consideration, with the end of well-doing, and not

of well-knowing only." If then virtuous action be the ultimate object of all our intellectual endeavours, can it be shown that the poet contributes above all others to this exalted aim? Sidney thinks it can.

Omitting divines and jurists, for obvious reasons, he finds that the poet's only competitors are philosophers and historians. It therefore now behoves him to prove that poetry contributes more to the formation of character for virtuous action than either philosophy or history. The argument is skilfully conducted, and developed with nice art; but it amounts in short to this, that while philosophy is too abstract and history is too concrete, poetry takes the just path between these extremes, and combines their methods in a harmony of more persuasive force than either. "Now doth the peerless poet perform both; for whatsoever the philosopher saith should be done, he giveth a perfect picture of it, by some one whom he presupposeth it was done, so as he coupleth the general notion with the particular example." "Anger, the Stoics said, was a short madness; but let Sophocles bring you Ajax on a stage, killing or whipping sheep and oxen, thinking them the army of Greeks, with their chieftains Agamemnon and Menelaus; and tell me if you have not a more familiar insight into anger than finding in the schoolmen his genus and difference?" Even Christ used parables and fables for the firmer inculcation of his divine precepts. If philosophy is too much occupied with the universal, history is too much bound to the particular. It dares not go beyond what was, may not travel into what might or should be. Moreover, "history being captivated to the truth of a foolish world, is many times a terror from well-doing,

and an encouragment to unbridled wickedness." It cannot avoid revealing virtue overwhelmed with calamity
and vice in prosperous condition. Poetry labours not
under the same restrictions. Her ideals, delightfully
presented, entering the soul with the enchanting strains
of music, " set the mind forward to that which deserves
to be called and accounted good." In fine : "as virtue
is the most excellent resting-place for all worldly learning to make his end of, so poetry, being the most familiar
to teach it, and most princely to move towards it, in the
most excellent work is the most excellent workman."

Sidney next passes the various species of poems in
review : the pastoral ; " the lamenting elegiac ;" " the
bitter but wholesome iambic ;" the satiric ; the comic,
" whom naughty play-makers and stage-keepers have
justly made odious ;" " the high and excellent tragedy,
that openeth the greatest wounds, and showeth forth the
ulcers that are covered with tissue—that maketh kings
fear to be tyrants, and tyrants to manifest their tyranni-
cal humours—that with stirring the effects of admiration and commiseration, teacheth the uncertainty of this
world, and upon how weak foundations gilded roofs are
builded ;" the lyric, "who with his tuned lyre and
well-accorded voice giveth praise, the reward of virtue,
to virtuous acts—who giveth moral precepts and natural
problems—who sometimes raiseth up his voice to the
height of the heavens, in singing the lauds of the immortal God ;" the epic or heroic, "whose very name, I
think, should daunt all backbiters . . . which is not
only a kind, but the best and most accomplished kind of
poetry." He calls upon the detractors of poesy to bring
their complaints against these several sorts, and to indi-

cate in each of them its errors. What they may allege
in disparagement, he meets with chosen arguments, among
which we can select his apology for the lyric. "Certainly, I must confess my own barbarousness : I never
heard the old song of 'Percy and Douglas' that I
found not my heart moved more than with a trumpet ;
and yet it is sung but by some blind crowder, with no
rougher voice than rude style ; which being so evil-
apparelled in the dust and cobweb of that uncivil age,
what would it work, trimmed in the gorgeous eloquence
of Pindar ?"

Having reached this point, partly on the way of
argument, partly on the path of appeal and persuasion,
Sidney halts to sum his whole position up in one condensed paragraph :

"Since, then, poetry is of all human learnings the most
ancient, and of most fatherly antiquity, as from whence other
learnings have taken their beginnings ; since it is so universal that no learned nation doth despise it, nor barbarous
nation is without it ; since both Roman and Greek gave such
divine names unto it, the one of prophesying, the other of
making, and that indeed that name of making is fit for him,
considering, that where all other arts retain themselves within their subject, and receive, as it were, their being from
it, the poet only, only bringeth his own stuff, and doth not
learn a conceit out of a matter, but maketh matter for a conceit ; since neither his description nor end containeth any
evil, the thing described cannot be evil ; since his effects be
so good as to teach goodness, and delight the learners of it ;
since therein (namely in moral doctrine, the chief of all know-
ledges) he doth not only far pass the historian, but, for in-
structing, is well nigh comparable to the philosopher ; for
moving, leaveth him behind him ; since the Holy Scripture
(wherein there is no uncleanness) hath whole parts in it
poetical, and that even our Saviour Christ vouchsafed to use

the flowers of it; since all his kinds are not only in their united forms, but in their severed dissections fully commendable; I think, and think I think rightly, the laurel crown appointed for triumphant captains, doth worthily, of all other learnings, honour the poet's triumph."

Objections remain to be combated in detail. Sidney chooses one first, which offers no great difficulty. The detractors of poetry gird at "rhyming and versing." He has already laid it down that "one may be a poet without versing, and a versifier without poetry." But he has also shown why metrical language should be regarded as the choicest and most polished mode of speech. Verse, too, fits itself to music more properly than prose, and far exceeds it "in the knitting up of the memory." Nor is rhyme to be neglected, especially in modern metres; seeing that it strikes a music to the ear. But the enemy advances heavier battalions. Against poetry he alleges (1) that there are studies upon which a man may spend his time more profitably; (2) that it is the mother of lies; (3) that it is the nurse of abuse, corrupting the fancy, enfeebling manliness, and instilling pestilent desires into the soul; (4) that Plato banished poets from his commonwealth.

These four points are taken seriatim, and severally answered. The first is set aside, as involving a begging of the question at issue. To the second Sidney replies " paradoxically, but truly I think truly, that of all writers under the sun the poet is the least liar; and though he would, as a poet, can scarcely be a liar." It is possible to err, and to affirm falsehood, in all the other departments of knowledge; but "for the poet, he nothing affirmeth, and therefore nothing lieth." His sphere is not the region of ascertained fact, or of logical propositions, but of imagination and invention. He labours not "to tell you what is, or is not, but what should, or should not be." None is so foolish as to mistake the poet's world for literal fact. " What child is there, that cometh to a play, and seeing Thebes written in great letters upon an old door, doth believe that it is Thebes?" The third point is more weighty. Are poets blamable, in that they "abuse men's wit, training it to a wanton sinfulness and lustful love?" Folk say "the comedies rather teach than reprehend amorous conceits; they say the lyric is larded with passionate sonnets; the elegiac weeps the want of his mistress; and that even to the heroical Cupid hath ambitiously climbed." Here Sidney turns to Love, and, as though himself acknowledging that deity, invokes him to defend his own cause. Yet let us "grant love of beauty to be a beastly fault," let us "grant that lovely name of love to deserve all hateful reproaches," what have the adversaries gained? Surely they have not proved "that poetry abuseth man's wit, but that man's wit abuseth poetry." "But what! shall the abuse of a thing make the right odious?" Does not law, does not physic, injure man every day by the abuse of ignorant practisers? "Doth not God's Word abused breed heresy, and His name abused become blasphemy?" Yet these people contend that before poetry came to infect the English, "our nation had set their heart's delight upon action and not imagination, rather doing things worthy to be written than writing things fit to be done." But when was there that time when the Albion nation was without poetry? Of a truth, this argument is levelled against all learning and all culture. It is an attack, worthy of Goths or Vandals, upon the stronghold of the intellect. As such, we might dismiss it. Let us, however, remember that "poetry is the companion of camps : I dare undertake, Orlando Furioso or honest King Arthur will never displease a soldier ; but the quiddity of *ens* and *prima materia* will hardly agree with a corselet." Alexander on his Indian campaigns left the living Aristotle behind him, but slept with the dead Homer in his tent; condemned Callisthenes to death, but yearned for a poet to commemorate his deeds. Lastly, they advance Plato's verdict against poets. Plato, says Sidney, "I have ever esteemed most worthy of reverence ; and with good reason, since of all philosophers he is the most poetical." Having delivered this sly thrust, he proceeds : "first, truly, a man might maliciously object that Plato, being a philosopher, was a natural enemy of poets." Next let us look into his writings. Has any poet authorised filthiness more abominable than one can find in the "Phaedrus" and the "Symposium ?" "Again, a man might ask out of what commonwealth Plato doth banish them." It is in sooth one where the community of women is permitted; and "little should poetical sonnets be hurtful, when a man might have what woman he listed." After thus trifling with the subject, Sidney points out that Plato was not offended with poetry, but with the abuse of it. He objected to the crude theology and the monstrous ethics of the myth-makers. "So as Plato, banishing the abuse not the thing, not banishing it, but giving due honour to it, shall be our patron and not our adversary."

Once again he pauses, to recapitulate :

" Since the excellencies of poesy may be so easily and so
justly confirmed, and the low creeping objections so soon
trodden down ; it not being an art of lies, but of true doctrine ;
not of effeminateness, but of notable stirring of courage ; not
of abusing man's wit, but of strengthening man's wit ; not
banished, but honoured by Plato ; let us rather plant more
laurels for to ingarland the poets' heads (which honour of
being laureate, as besides them only triumphant captains were,
is a sufficient authority to show the price they ought to be
held in) than suffer the ill-favoured breath of such wrong
speakers once to blow upon the clear springs of poesy."

Then he turns to England. Why is it that England,
"the mother of excellent minds, should be grown so
hard a stepmother to poets?"

"Sweet poesy, that hath anciently had kings, emperors,
senators, great captains, such as, besides a thousand others,
David, Adrian, Sophocles, Germanicus, not only to favour
poets, but to be poets : and of our nearer times, can present
for her patrons, a Robert, King of Sicily ; the great King
Francis of France ; King James of Scotland ; such cardinals
as Bembus and Bibiena ; such famous preachers and teachers
as Beza and Melancthon; so learned philosophers as Fracastorius
and Scaliger ; so great orators as Pontanus and Muretus ; so
piercing wits as George Buchanan ; so grave counsellors as,
besides many, but before all, that Hospital of France ; than
whom, I think, that realm never brought forth a more
accomplished judgment more firmly builded upon virtue ; I
say, these, with numbers of others, not only to read others'
poesies, but to poetise for others' reading : that poesy, thus
embraced in all other places, should only find, in our time, a
hard welcome in England, I think the very earth laments it,
and therefore decks our soil with fewer laurels than it was
accustomed."

The true cause is that in England so many incapable folk
write verses.   With the exception of the *Mirror of Magistrates*, Lord Surrey's Lyrics, and *The Shepherd's Kalendar*,

"I do not remember to have seen but few (to speak boldly) printed, that have poetical sinews in them." At this point he introduces a lengthy digression upon the stage, which, were we writing a history of the English drama, ought to be quoted in full. It is interesting because it proves how the theatre occupied Sidney's thoughts; and yet he had not perceived that from the humble plays of the people an unrivalled flower of modern art was about to emerge. *The Defence of Poesy* was written before Marlowe created the romantic drama; before Shakespeare arrived in London. It was written in all probability before its author could have attended the representation of Greene's and Peele's best plays. *Gorboduc*, which he praises moderately and censures with discrimination, seemed to him the finest product of dramatic art in England, because it approached the model of Seneca and the Italian tragedians. For the popular stage, with its chaos of tragic and comic elements, its undigested farrago of romantic incidents and involved plots, he entertained the scorn of a highly-educated scholar and a refined gentleman. Yet no one, let us be sure, would have welcomed *Othello* and *The Merchant of Venice*, *Volpone* and *A Woman Killed with Kindness*, more enthusiastically than Sidney, had his life been protracted through the natural span of mortality.

Having uttered his opinion frankly on the drama, he attacks the "courtesan-like painted affectation" of the English at his time. Far-fetched words, alliteration, euphuistic similes from stones and beasts and plants, fall under his honest censure. He mentions no man. But he is clearly aiming at the school of Lyly and the pedants; for he pertinently observes: "I have found in divers small-learned courtiers a more sound style than in some professors of learning." Language should be used, not to trick out thoughts with irrelevant ornaments or to smother them in conceits, but to make them as clear and natural as words can do. It is a sin against our mother speech to employ these meretricious arts ; for whoso will look dispassionately into the matter, shall convince himself that English, both in its freedom from inflections and its flexibility of accent, is aptest of all modern tongues to be the vehicle of simple and of beautiful utterance.

The peroration to *The Defence of Poesy* is an argument addressed to the personal ambition of the reader. It somewhat falls below the best parts of the essay in style, and makes no special claim on our attention. From the foregoing analysis it will be seen that Sidney attempted to cover a wide field, combining a philosophy of art with a practical review of English literature. Much as the Italians had recently written upon the theory of poetry, I do not remember any treatise which can be said to have supplied the material or suggested the method of this apology. England, of course, at that time was destitute of all but the most meagre textbooks on the subject. Great interest therefore attaches to Sidney's discourse as the original outcome of his studies, meditations, literary experience, and converse with men of parts. Though we may not be prepared to accept each of his propositions, though some will demur to his conception of the artist's moral aim, and others to his inclusion of prose fiction in the definition of poetry, while all will agree in condemning his mistaken dramatic theory, none can dispute the ripeness, mellowness, harmony, and felicity of mental gifts displayed in work at once so concise and so compendious.

It is indeed a pity that English literature then furnished
but slender material for criticism.   When we remember
that, among the poems of the English Renaissance, only
Surrey's Lyrics, *Gorboduc*, the *Mirror of Magistrates*, and
The Shepherd's Kalendar could be praised with candour
(and I think Sidney was right in this judgment), we shall
be better able to estimate his own high position, and our
mental senses will be dazzled by the achievements of the
last three centuries.   Exactly three centuries have elapsed
since Sidney fell at Zutphen; and who shall count the
poets of our race, stars differing indeed in glory, but stars
that stream across the heavens of song from him to us
in one continuous galaxy?

Sir Philip Sidney was not only eminent as pleader,
critic, and poet.   He also ranked as the patron and protector of men of letters.   "He was of a very munificent
spirit," says Aubrey, "and liberal to all lovers of learning,
and to those that pretended to any acquaintance with
Parnassus; insomuch that he was cloyed and surfeited
with the poetasters of those days."   This sentence is
confirmed by the memorial verses written on his death,
and by the many books which were inscribed with his
name.   A list of these may be read in Dr. Zouch's *Life*.
It is enough for our purpose to enumerate the more
distinguished.   To Sidney, Spenser dedicated the first
fruits of his genius, and Hakluyt the first collection of
his epoch-making Voyages.   Henri Etienne, who was
proud to call himself the friend of Sidney, placed his
1576 edition of the Greek Testament and his 1581
edition of Herodian under the protection of his name.
Lord Brooke, long after his friend's death, dedicated his
collected works to Sidney's memory.

Of all these tributes to his love of learning the most
interesting in my opinion is that of Giordano Bruno.
This Titan of impassioned speculation passed two years
in London between 1583 and 1585. Here he composed,
and here he printed, his most important works in the
Italian tongue. Two of these he presented, with
pompous commendatory epistles, to Sir Philip Sidney.
They were his treatise upon Ethics, styled *Lo Spaccio
della Bestia Trionfante*, and his discourse upon the philo-
sophic enthusiasm, entitled *Gli Eroici Furori*. That
Bruno belonged to Sidney's circle, is evident from the
graphic account he gives of a supper at Fulke Greville's
house, in the dialogue called *La Cena delle Ceneri*. His
appreciation of "the most illustrious and excellent
knight's" character transpires in the following phrase
from one of his dedications : "the natural bias of your
spirit, which is truly heroical." Those who know what
the word *eroica* implied for Bruno, not only of personal
courage, but of sustained and burning spiritual passion,
will appreciate this eulogy by one of the most pene-
trating and candid, as he was the most unfortunate
of truth's martyrs. Had the proportions of my work
justified such a digression, I would eagerly have collected
from Bruno's Italian discourses those paragraphs which
cast a vivid light upon literary and social life in England.
But these belong rather to Bruno's than to Sidney's
biography.

CHAPTER VIII

LAST YEARS AND DEATH

AFTER Sidney's marriage there remained but little more than three years of life to him. The story of this period may be briefly told. Two matters of grave import occupied his mind. These were; first, the menacing attitude of Spain and the advance of the Counter-Reformation; secondly, a project of American Colonisation. The suspicious death of the Duke of Anjou, followed by the murder of the Prince of Orange in 1584, rendered Elizabeth's interference in the Low Countries almost imperative. Philip II., assisted by the powers of Catholicism, and served in secret by the formidable Company of Jesus, threatened Europe with the extinction of religious and political liberties. It was known that, sooner or later, he must strike a deadly blow at England. The Armada loomed already in the distance. But how was he to be attacked? Sidney thought that Elizabeth would do well to put herself at the head of a Protestant alliance against what Fulke Greville aptly styled the "masked triplicity between Spain, Rome, and the Jesuitical faction of France." He also strongly recommended an increase of the British navy and a policy of protecting the Huguenots in their French seaports. But he judged

the Netherlands an ill-chosen field for fighting the main
duel out with Spain. There, Philip was firmly seated
in well-furnished cities, where he could mass troops and
munitions of war at pleasure. To maintain an opposition on the side of Holland was of course necessary.
But the really vulnerable point in the huge Spanish
empire seemed to him to be its ill-defended territory in
the West Indies. Let then the Protestant League, if
possible, be placed upon a firmer basis. Let war in the
Low Countries be prosecuted without remission. But,
at the same time, let the English use their strongest
weapon, attack by sea. Descents might be made from
time to time upon the Spanish ports, as Drake had
already harried Vera Cruz, and was afterwards to fall
on Cadiz. Buccaneering and filibustering expeditions
against the Spanish fleets which brought back treasure
across the Indian main, were not to be contemned.
But he believed that the most efficient course would be
to plant a colony upon the American continent, which
should at the same time be a source of strength to
England and a hostile outpost for incursions into the
Spanish settlements. Fulke Greville has devoted a
large portion of his *Life* to the analysis of Sidney's
opinions on these subjects. He sums them up as
follows: "Upon these and the like assumptions he
resolved there were but two ways left to frustrate this
ambitious monarch's designs. The one, that which
diverted Hannibal, and by setting fire on his own house
made him draw in his spirits to comfort his heart; the
other, that of Jason, by fetching away his golden fleece
and not suffering any one man quietly to enjoy that
which every man so much affected."

In the autumn of 1584 Sidney sat again in the House
of Commons, where he helped to forward the bill for
Raleigh's expedition to Virginia. This in fact was an
important step in the direction of his favourite scheme ;
for his view of the American colony was that it should
be a real " plantation, not like an asylum for fugitives,
a *bellum piraticum* for banditti, or any such base *ramas*
of people ; but as an emporium for the confluence of all
nations that love or profess any kind of virtue or
commerce." Parliament next year had to take strong
measures against the Jesuits, who were already foment-
ing secret conspiracies to dethrone or assassinate the
queen. The session ended in March, and in April
Raleigh started for the New World. Three months
later Sidney received a commission to share the Mastership of the Ordnance with his uncle Warwick. He
found that department of the public service in a
lamentable plight, owing to Elizabeth's parsimony ; and
soon after his appointment, he risked her displeasure
by firmly pressing for a thorough replenishment of the
stores upon which England's efficiency as a belligerent
would depend.

It was probably in this year that Sidney took
up his pen to defend his uncle Leicester against the
poisonous libel, popularly known as *Leicester's Commonwealth*, and generally ascribed to the Jesuit Parsons.
We possess the rough draft of his discourse, which
proves convincingly that he at least was persuaded of
the earl's innocence. He does not even deign to answer
the charges of "dissimulation, hypocrisy, adultery,
falsehood, treachery, poison, rebellion, treason, cowar-
dice, atheism, and what not," except by a flat denial,

and a contemptuous interrogation : "what is it else but such a bundle of railings, as if it came from the mouth of some half-drunk scold in a tavern?" By far the larger portion of the defence is occupied with an elaborate exhibition of the pedigree and honours of the House of Dudley, in reply to the hint that Edmund, Leicester's grandfather, was basely born. Sidney, as we have seen, set great store on his own descent from the Dudleys, which he rated higher than his paternal ancestry; and this aspersion on their origin inspired him with un-measured anger. At the close of the pamphlet he throws down the glove to his anonymous antagonist, and defies him to single combat. "And, from the date of this writing, imprinted and published, I will three months expect thine answer." Horace Walpole was certainly not justified in calling this spirited, but ill-balanced composition "by far the best specimen of his abilities."

June 1585 marked an era in the foreign policy of Elizabeth. She received a deputation from the Nether-lands, who offered her the sovereignty of the United Provinces if she would undertake their cause. This offer she refused. But the recent adhesion of the French Crown to what was called the Holy League, rendered it necessary that she should do something. Accordingly, she agreed to send 6000 men to the Low Countries, holding Flushing and Brill with the Castle of Ram-mekins in pledge for the repayment of the costs of this expedition. Sidney began now to be spoken of as the most likely governor of Flushing. But at this moment his thoughts were directed rather to the New World than to action in Flanders. We have already

seen why he believed it best to attack Spain there. A
letter written to him by Ralph Lane from Virginia
echoes his own views upon this topic. The governor of
the new plantation strongly urged him to head a force
against what Greville called " that rich and desert West
Indian mine." Passing by the islands of St. John and
Hispaniola, Lane had observed their weakness. " How
greatly a small force would garboil him here, when two
of his most richest and strongest islands took such
alarms of us, not only landing, but dwelling upon them,
with only a hundred and twenty men, I refer it to your
judgment." Sidney, moreover, had grown to distrust
Burleigh's government of England. " Nature," says
Greville, " guiding his eyes first to his native country,
he found greatness of worth and place counterpoised
there by the arts of power and favour. The stirring
spirits sent abroad as fuel, to keep the flame far off ;
and the effeminate made judges of dangers which they
fear, and honour which they understand not." He saw
" how the idle-censuring faction at home had won ground
of the active adventurers abroad ; " he perceived the
queen's " governors to sit at home in their soft chairs,
playing fast and loose with them that ventured their
lives abroad." All these considerations put together
made him more than lukewarm about the Netherlands
campaign and less than eager to take office under so
egotistical an administration. It was his cherished
scheme to join in some private enterprise, the object of
which should be the enfeeblement of Spain and the
strengthening of England beyond the Atlantic.

The thoughts which occupied his mind took definite
shape in the summer of 1585. " The next step which

he intended into the world was an expedition of his
own projecting; wherein he fashioned the whole body,
with purpose to become head of it himself. I mean the
last employment but one of Sir Francis Drake to the
West Indies." With these words Greville introduces a
minute account of Sidney's part in that famous adventure. He worked hard at the project, stirring up the
several passions which might induce men of various
sympathies to furnish assistance by money or by personal
participation.

"To martial men he opened wide the door of sea and
land for fame and conquest. To the nobly ambitious, the
far stage of America to win honour in. To the religious
divines, besides a new apostolical calling of the lost heathen
to the Christian faith, a large field of reducing poor Christians
misled by the idolatry of Rome to their mother primitive
church. To the ingeniously industrious, variety of natural
riches for new mysteries and manufactures to work upon.
To the merchant, with a simple people a fertile and unex-
hausted earth. To the fortune-bound, liberty. To the
curious, a fruitful work of innovation. Generally, the word
gold was an attractive adamant to make men venture that
which they have in hope to grow rich by that which they
have not."

Moreover he "won thirty gentlemen of great blood and
state here in England, every man to sell one hundred
pounds land" for fitting out a fleet. While firmly resolved to join the first detachment which should sail
from Plymouth, he had to keep his plans dark; for the
queen would not hear of his engaging in such ventures.
It was accordingly agreed between him and Sir Francis
that the latter should go alone to Plymouth, and that
Sir Philip should meet him there upon some plausible

excuse. When they had weighed anchor, Sidney was to
share the chief command with Drake. Sir Francis in
due course of time set off; and early in September
he sent a message praying urgently for his associate's
presence. It so happened that just at this time Don
Antonio of Portugal was expected at Plymouth, and
Philip obtained leave to receive him there. From this
point I shall let Fulke Greville tell the story in his own
old-fashioned language :—

"Yet I that had the honour, as of being bred with him
from his youth, so now by his own choice of all England to
be his loving and beloved Achates in this journey, observing
the countenance of this gallant mariner more exactly than Sir
Philip's leisure served him to do, after we were laid in bed
acquainted him with my observation of the discountenance
and depression which appeared in Sir Francis, as if our
coming were both beyond his expectation and desire.
Nevertheless that ingenuous spirit of Sir Philip's, though apt
to give me credit, yet not apt to discredit others, made him
suspend his own and labour to change or qualify by judgment ; till within some few days after, finding the ships
neither ready according to promise, nor possibly to be made
ready in many days, and withal observing some sparks of
false fire breaking out from his yoke-fellow daily, it pleased
him in the freedom of our friendship to return me my own
stock with interest.

"All this while Don Antonio landed not ; the fleet seemed
to us, like the weary passengers' inn, still to go farther from
our desires ; letters came from the Court to hasten it away ;
but it may be the leaden feet and nimble thoughts of Sir
Francis wrought in the day, and unwrought by night, while
he watched an opportunity to discover us without being discovered.

"For within a few days after, a post steals up to the
Court, upon whose arrival an alarm is presently taken :
messengers sent away to stay us, or if we refused, to stay the
whole fleet. Notwithstanding this first Mercury, his errand

being partly advertised to Sir Philip beforehand, was intercepted upon the way ; his letters taken from him by two resolute soldiers in mariners' apparel, brought instantly to Sir Philip, opened and read. The next was a more imperial mandate, carefully conveyed and delivered to himself by a peer of this realm ; carrying with it in the one hand grace, the other thunder. The grace was an offer of an instant employment under his uncle, then going general into the Low Countries ; against which as though he would gladly have demurred, yet the confluence of reason, transcendency of power, fear of staying the whole fleet, made him instantly sacrifice all these self-places to the duty of obedience."

In plain words, then, Sir Francis Drake, disliking the prospect of an equal in command, played Sir Philip Sidney false by sending private intelligence to Court. The queen expressed her will so positively that Sidney had to yield. At the same time it was settled that he should go into the Netherlands, under his uncle Leicester, holding her Majesty's commission as Governor of Flushing and Rammekins. By this rapid change of events his destiny was fixed. Drake set sail on the 14th of September. Two months later, on the 16th of November, Sidney left England for his post in the Low Countries. I ought here to add that at some time during this busy summer his daughter, Elizabeth, afterwards Countess of Rutland, was born.

Sidney's achievements in the Netherlands, except as forming part of his short life, claim no particular attention. He was welcomed by Count Maurice of Nassau, the eldest son of William, Prince of Orange ; and gleanings from letters of the time show that folk expected much from his activity and probity. But he enjoyed narrow scope for the employment of his abilities. Rammekins, the fortress which commanded Flushing, was inadequately furnished and badly garrisoned. The troops were insufficient, and so ill-paid that mutinies were always imminent. In one of his despatches, urgently demanding fresh supplies, he says : "I am in a garrison as much able to command Flushing as the Tower is to answer for London." The Dutch government did not please him : he found "the people far more careful than the government in all things touching the public welfare." With the plain speech that was habitual to him, he demanded more expenditure of English money. This irritated the queen, and gave his enemies at Court occasion to condemn him in his absence as ambitious and proud. He began to show signs of impatience with Elizabeth. "If her Majesty were the fountain, I would fear, considering what I daily find, that we should wax dry." This bitter taunt he vented in a letter to Sir Francis Walsingham. Meanwhile the Earl of Leicester arrived upon the 10th of December, and made matters worse. He laid himself out for honours of all sorts, accepting the title of Governor-General over the United Provinces, and coquetting with some vague scheme of being chosen for their sovereign. Imposing but impotent, Leicester had no genius for military affairs. The winter of 1585-86 dragged through, with nothing memorable to relate.

The following season, however, was marked by several important incidents in Philip Sidney's private life. First, Lady Sidney joined her husband at Flushing. Then on the 5th of May Sir Henry Sidney died in the bishop's palace at Worcester. His body was embalmed and sent to Penshurst. His heart was buried at Ludlow; his entrails in the precincts of Worcester Cathedral.

So passed from life Elizabeth's sturdy servant in Ireland and Wales; a man, as I conceive him, of somewhat limited capacity and stubborn temper, but true as steel, and honest in the discharge of very trying duties. Later in the same year, upon the 9th of August, Lady Mary Sidney yielded up her gentle spirit. Of her there is nothing to be written but the purest panegyric. Born of the noblest blood, surviving ambitious relatives who reached at royalty and perished, losing health and beauty in the service of an exacting queen, suffering poverty at Court, supporting husband and children through all trials with wise counsel and sweet hopeful temper, she emerges with pale lustre from all the actors of that time to represent the perfect wife and mother in a lady of unpretending, but heroic, dignity. Sidney would have been the poorer for the loss of these parents, if his own life had been spared. As it was, he survived his mother but two months.

In July he distinguished himself by the surprise and capture of the little town of Axel. Leicester rewarded him for this service with the commission of colonel. Elizabeth resented his promotion. She wished the colonelcy for Count Hohenlohe, or Hollock, a brave but drunken soldier. Walsingham wrote upon the occasion: "She layeth the blame upon Sir Philip, as a thing by him ambitiously sought. I see her Majesty very apt upon every light occasion to find fault with him." Ambition, not of the vaulting kind, which "overleaps itself," but of a steady, persistent, intellectual stamp, was, indeed, I think, the leading quality in Sidney's nature. From the courtiers of the period, the Leicesters, Oxfords, Ormonds, Hattons, and so forth,

this mark of character honourably distinguished him.
And, if he had but lived, Elizabeth, who judged her
servants with some accuracy, might by judicious curbing
and parsimonious encouragement have tempered the fine
steel of his frailty into a blade of trenchant edge.
There was nothing ignoble, nothing frivolous in his ambition.   It was rather of such mettle as made the heroes
of the commonwealth : pure and un-self-seeking, but
somewhat acrid.   And now he fretted himself too much
because of evil-doers ; impatiently demanded men and
munitions from England ; vented his bile in private
letters against Leicester.   Sidney was justified by events.
The campaign dragged negligently on ; and the Com-
mander of the Forces paid more attention to banquets
and diplomatic intrigues than to the rough work of war.
But the tone adopted by him in his irritation was hardly
prudent for so young and so comparatively needy a
gentleman.

Whatever he found to blame in Leicester's conduct
of affairs, Sidney did not keep aloof ; but used every
effort to inspire his uncle with some of his own spirit.
At the end of August they were both engaged in reducing the little fort of Doesburg on the Yssel, which had
importance as the key to Zutphen.   It fell upon the 2d
of September ; and on the 13th Zutphen was invested—
Lewis William of Nassau, Sir John Norris, and Sir
Philip Sidney commanding the land-forces, and Leicester
blockading the approach by water.   The Duke of Parma,
acting for Spain, did all he could to reinforce the garrison with men and provisions.   News came upon the 21st
to Leicester that a considerable convoy was at Deventer
waiting an opportunity to enter the town.   He resolved

to cut off these supplies, and fixed an early hour of the
22d, which was a Thursday, for this operation. We
have a letter, the last which Sidney penned before his
fatal wound, dated from the camp at Zutphen upon the
morning of the engagement. It recommends Richard
Smyth, "her Majesty's old servant," to Sir Francis
Walsingham, and is one among several writings of the
kind which show how mindful Sidney was of humble
friends and people in distress. The 22d of September
opened gloomily. So thick a mist covered the Flemish
lowlands that a man could not see farther than ten
paces. Sidney, leading a troop of two hundred horsemen, pushed his way up to the walls of Zutphen.
Chivalrous punctilio caused him to be ill-defended, for
meeting Sir William Pelham in light armour, he threw
off his cuisses, and thus exposed himself to unnecessary
danger. The autumn fog, which covered every object,
suddenly dispersed; and the English now found themselves confronted by a thousand horsemen of the enemy,
and exposed to the guns of the town. They charged,
and Sidney's horse was killed under him. He mounted
another, and joined in the second charge. Reinforce-
ments came up, and a third charge was made, during
which he received a wound in the left leg. The bullet,
which some supposed to have been poisoned, entered
above the knee, broke the bone, and lodged itself high
up in the thigh. His horse took fright, and carried him
at a gallop from the field. He kept his seat, however;
and when the animal was brought to order, had himself
carried to Leicester's station. On the way occurred the
incident so well-known to every one who is acquainted
with his name. "Being thirsty with excess of bleeding,

he called for drink, which was presently brought him ; but as he was putting the bottle to his mouth, he saw a poor soldier carried along, who had eaten his last at the same feast, ghastly casting up his eyes at the bottle, which Sir Philip perceiving, took it from his head before he drank, and delivered it to the poor man, with these words, *Thy necessity is yet greater than mine.* And when he had pledged this poor soldier, he was presently carried to Arnheim."

At Arnheim he lay twenty-five days in the house of a lady named Gruitthueisens. At first the surgeons who attended him had good hopes of his recovery. Ten days after the event Leicester wrote to Walsingham : " All the worst days be passed, and he amends as well as possible in this time." Friends were around him—his wife, his brothers Robert and Thomas, and the excellent minister, George Gifford, whom he sent for on the 30th. The treatment of the wound exposed him to long and pain ful operations, which he bore with a sweet fortitude that moved the surgeons to admiration. With Gifford and other godly men he held discourses upon religion and the future of the soul. He told Gifford that "he had walked in a vague course ; and these words he spake with great vehemence both of speech and gesture, and doubled it to the intent that it might be manifest how unfeignedly he meant to turn more thoughts unto God than ever." It is said that he amused some hours of tedious leisure by composing a poem on *La Cuisse Rompue*, which was afterwards sung to soothe him. He also contrived to write "a large epistle in very pure and eloquent Latin " to his friend Belarius the divine. Both of these are lost.

As time wore on it appeared that the cure was not advancing. After the sixteenth day, says Greville, "the very shoulder-bones of this delicate patient were worn through his skin." He suffered from sharp pangs which "stang him by fits," and felt internally that his case was desperate. "One morning lifting up the clothes for change and ease of his body, he smelt some extraordinary noisome savour about him, differing from oils and salves, as he conceived." This he judged, and judged rightly, to be the sign of "inward mortification, and a welcome messenger of death." Thereupon he called the ministers into his presence, "and before them made such a confession of Christian faith as no book but the heart can truly and feelingly deliver." Death had its terrors for his soul ; but he withstood them manfully, seeking peace and courage in the sacrifice of all earthly affections. "There came to my mind," he said to Gifford, "a vanity in which I delighted, whereof I had not rid myself. I rid myself of it, and presently my joy and comfort returned." Soon he was able to declare : "I would not change my joy for the empire of the world." Yet, up to the very last, he did not entirely despair of life. This is proved by the very touching letter he wrote to John Wier, a famous physician, and a friend of his. It runs thus in Latin : "Mi Wiere, veni, veni. De vitâ periclitor et te cupio. Nec vivus, nec mortuus, ero ingratus. Plura non possum, sed obnixe oro ut festines. Vale. Tuus Ph. Sidney." "My dear friend Wier, come, come. I am in peril of my life, and long for you. Neither living nor dead shall I be ungrateful. I cannot write more, but beg you urgently to hurry. Farewell. Your Ph. Sidney." In this way several days passed slowly on.

He had made his will upon the 30th of September. This he now revised, adding a codicil in which he remembered many friends and servants. The document may be read in Collins's *Sidney Papers*. Much of it is occupied with provisions for the child, with which his wife was pregnant at this time, and of which she was afterwards delivered still-born. But the thoughtful tenor of the whole justifies Greville in saying that it "will ever remain for a witness to the world that those sweet and large affections in him could no more be contracted with the narrowness of pain, grief, or sickness, than any sparkle of our immortality can be privately buried in the shadow of death.'

Reflecting upon the past he exclaimed : "All things in my former life have been vain, vain, vain." In this mood he bade one of his friends burn the *Arcadia ;* but we know not whether he expressed the same wish about *Astrophel and Stella.* On the morning of the 17th of October it was clear that he had but a few hours to live. His brother Robert gave way to passionate grief in his presence, which Philip gently stayed, taking farewell of him in these memorable words : " Love my memory, cherish my friends ; their faith to me may assure you they are honest. But above all, govern your will and affections by the will and word of your Creator ; in me beholding the end of this world with all her vanities." Shortly afterwards he sank into speechlessness, and the bystanders thought that what he had greatly dreaded—namely, death without consciousness, would befall him. Yet when they prayed him for some sign of his "inward joy and consolation in God," he held his hand up and stretched it forward for a little while. About two o'clock in the afternoon he again responded to a similar appeal by setting his hands together in the attitude of prayer upon his breast, and thus he expired.

Sidney's death sent a thrill through Europe. Leicester, who truly loved him, wrote upon the 25th, in words of passionate grief, to Walsingham. Elizabeth declared that she had lost her mainstay in the struggle with Spain. Duplessis Mornay bewailed his loss " not for England only, but for all Christendom." Mendoza, the Spanish secretary, said that though he could not but rejoice at the loss to his master of such a foe, he yet lamented to see Christendom deprived of so great a light, and bewailed poor widowed England. The Netherlanders begged to be allowed to keep his body, and promised to erect a royal monument to his memory, "yea, though the same should cost half-a-ton of gold in the building." But this petition was rejected ; and the corpse, after embalmment, was removed to Flushing. There it lay eight days ; and on the 1st of November the English troops accompanied it with military honours to the *Black Prince*, a vessel which had belonged to Sidney. On the 5th it reached Tower Hill, and on the 16th of February it was buried with pomp in St. Paul's. This long delay between the landing in London and the interment arose from certain legal complications, which rendered the discharge of Sidney's debts difficult. Walsingham told Leicester that he would have to " pay for him about six thousand pounds, which I do assure your Lordship hath brought me into a most desperate and hard state, which I weigh nothing in respect of the loss of the gentleman who was my chief worldly comfort." Lest this should seem to reflect ill upon Sidney's character, it must be added that he had furnished Walsingham with a power of attorney to sell land, and had expressly considered all his creditors in his will. But his own death happened so close upon his father's, and the will was so imperfect touching the sale of land, that his wishes could not be carried into effect. This, added Walsingham, "doth greatly afflict me, that a gentleman that hath lived so unspotted in reputation, and had so great care to see all men satisfied, should be so exposed to the outcry of his creditors." When the obstacles had been surmounted the funeral was splendid and public. And the whole nation went into mourning. "It was accounted a sin," says the author of *The Life and Death of Sir Philip Sidney*, "for any gentleman of quality, for many months after, to appear at Court or City in any light or gaudy apparel."

I have told the story of Sidney's last days briefly, using the testimony of those who knew him best, or who were present at his death-bed. Comment would be superfluous. There is a singular beauty in the uncomplaining, thoughtful, manly sweetness of the young hero cut off in his prime. Numberless minute touches, of necessity omitted here, confirm the opinion that Sidney possessed unique charm and exercised a spell over those who came in contact with him. All the letters and reports which deal with that long agony breathe a heartfelt tenderness, which proves how amiable and how admirable he was. The character must have been wellnigh perfect which inspired persons so different as the Earl of Leicester, George Gifford, and Fulke Greville with the same devoted love. We have not to deal merely with the record of an edifying end, but with the longing retrospect of men whose best qualities had been drawn forth by sympathy with his incomparable goodness.

The limits of this book make it impossible to give an adequate account of the multitudinous literary tributes to Sidney's memory, which appeared soon after his decease. Oxford contributed *Exequiae* and *Peplus;* Cambridge shed *Lacrymae;* great wits and little, to the number it is said of some two hundred, expressed their grief with more or less felicity of phrase. For us the value of these elegiac verses is not great. But it is of some importance to know what men of weight and judgment said of him. His dearest and best friend has been so often quoted in these pages that we are now familiar with Greville's life-long adoration. Yet I cannot omit the general character he gives of Sidney :

"Indeed he was a true model of worth ; a man fit for conquest, plantation, reformation, or what action soever is greatest and hardest among men : withal, such a lover of mankind and goodness that whoever had any real parts in him, found comfort, participation, and protection to the uttermost of his power : like Zephyrus, he giving life where he blew. The universities abroad and at home accounted him a general Mecaenas of learning ; dedicated their books to him ; and communicated every invention or improvement of knowledge with him. Soldiers honoured him, and were so honoured by him as no man thought he marched under the true banner of Mars that had not obtained Sir Philip Sidney's approbation. Men of affairs in most parts of Christendom entertained correspondency with him. But what speak I of these, with whom his own ways and ends did concur ? Since, to descend, his heart and capacity were so large that there was not a cunning painter, a skilful engineer, an excellent musician, or any other artificer of extraordinary fame, that made not himself known to this famous spirit, and found him his true friend without hire, and the common *rendezvous* of worth in his time."

Thomas Nash may be selected as the representative of literary men who honoured Sidney.

" Gentle Sir Philip Sidney ! " he exclaims ; " thou knewest what belonged to a scholar ; thou knewest what pains, what toil, what travail, conduct to perfection ; well couldst thou give every virtue his encouragement, every art his due, every writer his desert, cause none more virtuous, witty, or learned than thyself. But thou art dead in thy grave, and hast left too few successors of thy glory, too few to cherish the sons of the Muses, or water those budding hopes with their plenty, which thy bounty erst planted."

Lastly, we will lay the ponderous laurel-wreath, woven by grave Camden, on his tomb :

" This is that Sidney, who, as Providence seems to have sent him into the world to give the present age a specimen of the ancients, so did it on a sudden recall him, and snatch him from us, as more worthy of heaven than earth ; thus where virtue comes to perfection, it is gone in a trice, and the best things are never lasting. Rest then in peace, O Sidney, if I may be allowed this address ! We will not celebrate your memory with tears but admiration ; whatever we loved in you, as the best of authors speaks of that best governor of Britain, whatever we admired in you, still continues, and will continue in the memories of men, the revolutions of ages, and the annals of time. Many, as inglorious and ignoble, are buried in oblivion ; but Sidney shall live to all posterity. For, as the Grecian poet has it, virtue's beyond the reach of fate."

The note of tenderness, on which I have already dwelt, sounds equally in these sentences of the needy man of letters and the learned antiquarian.

It would be agreeable, if space permitted, to turn the

pages of famous poets who immortalised our hero; to
glean high thoughts from Constable's sonnets to Sir
Philip Sidney's soul; to dwell on Raleigh's well-weighed
quatrains; to gather pastoral honey from Spenser's
Astrophel, or graver meditations from his *Ruins of Time*.
But these are in the hands of every one; and now, at the
close of his biography, I will rather let the voice of
unpretending affection be heard. Few but students, I
suppose, are familiar with the name of Matthew Roydon,
or know that he was a writer of some distinction.
Perhaps it was love for Sidney which inspired him with
the musical but unequal poem from which I select three
stanzas:

> "Within these woods of Arcady
>   He chief delight and pleasure took;
> And on the mountain Partheny,
>   Upon the crystal liquid brook,
> The Muses met him every day,
> That taught him sing, to write and say.

> "When he descended down the mount,
>   His personage seemed most divine;
> A thousand graces one might count
>   Upon his lovely cheerful eyne.
> To hear him speak, and sweetly smile,
> You were in Paradise the while.

> "A sweet attractive kind of grace;
>   A full assurance given by looks;
> Continual comfort in a face;
>   The lineaments of Gospel books:
> I trow that countenance cannot lie,
> Whose thoughts are legible in the eye."

Among Spenser's works, incorporated in his *Astrophel*,
occurs an elegy of languid but attractive sweetness, which

the great poet ascribes to the Countess of Pembroke,
sister by blood to Sidney, and sister of his soul.   Internal
evidence might lead to the opinion that this "doleful lay
of Clorinda," as it is usually called, was not written by
Lady Pembroke, but was composed for her by the author
of the *Faery Queen*.   Yet the style is certainly inferior
to that of Spenser at its best, and critics of mark incline
to accept it literally as her production.   This shall serve
me as an excuse for borrowing some of its verses :

> "What cruel hand of cursèd foe unknown
>   Hath cropped the stalk which bore so fair a flower ?
> Untimely cropped, before it well were grown,
>   And clean defacèd in untimely hour !
> Great loss to all that ever him did see,
> Great loss to all, but greatest loss to me !

> "Break now your garlands, oh, ye shepherds' lasses,
>   Since the fair flower which them adorned is gone ;
> The flower which them adorned is gone to ashes ;
>   Never again let lass put garland on ;
> Instead of garland, wear sad cypress now,
> And bitter elder broken from the bough."

The reiteration of phrases in these softly-falling
stanzas recalls the plaining of thrush or blackbird in
the dewy silence of May evenings.   But at the close
of her long descant, Urania changes to thoughts of the
heaven whose light has been increased by the "fair and
glittering rays" of Astrophel.   Then her inspiration
takes a loftier flight.   Meditations are suggested which
prelude to *Lycidas* and *Adonais*.   A parallel, indeed,
both of diction and idea between this wilding flower
of song and the magnificent double-rose of Shelley's
threnody on Keats can be traced in the following four
stanzas :—

" But that immortal spirit, which was decked
  With all the dowries of celestial grace,
By sovereign choice from the heavenly choirs select,
  And lineally derived from angel's race,
Oh, what is now of it become, aread !
Ah me, can so divine a thing be dead ?

" Ah no ! it is not dead, nor can it die,
  But lives for aye in blissful paradise,
Where, like a new-born babe it soft doth lie,
  In beds of lilies wrapped in tender wise,
And compassed all about with roses sweet
And dainty violets from head to feet.

" There lieth he in everlasting bliss,
  Sweet spirit, never fearing more to die ;
Nor dreading harm from any foes of his,
  Nor fearing savage beasts' more cruelty :
Whilst we here, wretches, wail his private lack,
And with vain vows do often call him back.

" But live thou there still, happy, happy spirit,
  And give us leave thee here thus to lament,
Not thee that dost thy heaven's joy inherit,
  But our own selves that here in dole are drent.
Thus do we weep and wail and wear our eyes,
Mourning in others our own miseries."

One couplet by a nameless playwright upon the death
of Sidney's aunt by marriage, the Lady Jane Grey, shall
serve to end this chapter :

> " An innocent to die, what is it less
>   But to add angels to heaven's happiness ! "

EPILOGUE

WHEN we review the life of Sir Philip Sidney, it is
certain that one thought will survive all other thoughts

about him in our mind. This man, we shall say, was
born to show the world what goes to the making of an
English gentleman. But he belonged to his age; and
the age of Elizabeth differed in many essential qualities
from the age of Anne and from the age of Victoria.
Sidney was the typical English gentleman of the modern
era at the moment of transition from the mediæval
period. He was the hero of our Renaissance. His
nature combined chivalry and piety, courtly breeding
and humane culture, statesmanship and loyalty, in what
Wotton so well called "the very essence of congruity."
Each of these elements may be found singly and more
strikingly developed in other characters of his epoch.
In him they were harmoniously mixed and fused as by
some spiritual chemistry. In him they shone with a
lustre peculiar to the "spacious times of great Elizabeth,"
with a grace and purity distinctive of his unique personality. To make this image charming—this image, not
of king or prince or mighty noble, but of a perfect
gentleman—the favour of illustrious lineage and the
grave beauty of his presence contributed in no small
measure. There was something Phœbean in his youthful
dignity :

> "When he descended down the mount,
>   His personage seemed most divine."

Men of weight and learning were reminded by him of
the golden antique past : "Providence seems to have
sent him into the world to give the present age a
specimen of the ancients." What the Athenians called
καλοκαγαθία, that blending of physical and moral beauty
and goodness in one pervasive virtue, distinguished him

from the crowd of his countrymen, with whom goodness
too often assumed an outer form of harshness and
beauty leaned to effeminacy or insolence.   He gave
the present age a specimen of the ancients by the
plasticity of his whole nature, the exact correspondence
of spiritual and corporeal excellences, which among
Greeks would have marked him out for sculpturesque
idealisation.

It was to his advantage that he held no office of
importance, commanded no great hereditary wealth, had
done no deeds that brought him envy, had reached no
station which committed him to rough collision with the
world's brazen interests.   Death, and the noble manner
of his death, set seal to the charter of immortality which
the expectation of contemporaries had already drafted.
He was withdrawn from the contention of our earth,
before time and opportunity proved or compromised his
high position.   Gloriously, he passed into the sphere of
idealities ; and as an ideal, he is for ever living and for
ever admirable.   Herein too there was something Greek
in his good fortune ; something which assimilates him
to the eternal youthfulness of Hellas, and to the adoles-
cent heroes of mythology.

This should not divert our thoughts from the fact
that Sidney was essentially an Elizabethan gentleman.
His chivalry belonged to a period when knightly
exercises were still in vogue, when bravery attired
itself in pomp, when the Mort d'Arthur retained its
fascination for youths of noble nurture.   Those legends
needed then no adaptations from a Laureate's golden
quill to make them popular.   Yet they were remote
enough to touch the soul with poetry, of which the

earlier and cruder associations had by time been mellowed. Knight-errantry expressed itself in careers like that of Stukeley, in expeditions like those of Drake and Raleigh. Lancelot's and Tristram's love had passed through the crucible of the Italian poets.

Sidney's piety was that of the Reformation, now at length accomplished and accepted in England after a severe struggle. Unsapped by criticism, undimmed by centuries of ease and toleration, the Anglican faith acquired reality and earnestness from the gravity of the European situation. Spain threatened to enslave the world. The Catholic reaction was rolling spiritual darkness, like a cloud, northward, over nations wavering as yet between the old and the new creed. Four years before his birth Loyola founded the Company of Jesus. During his lifetime this Order invaded province after province, spreading like leaven through populations on the verge of revolt against Rome. The Council of Trent began its sessions while he was in his cradle. Its work was finished, the final rupture of the Latin Church with Protestantism was accomplished, twenty-three years before his death at Zutphen. He grew to boyhood during Mary's reactionary reign. It is well to bear these dates in mind; they prove how exactly Sidney's life corresponded with the first stage of renascent and belligerent Catholicism. The perils of the time, brought fearfully home to himself by his sojourn in Paris on the night of St. Bartholomew, deepened religious convictions which might otherwise have been but lightly held by him. Yet he was no Puritan. Protestantism in England had as yet hardly entered upon that phase of its development. It was still possible to be sincerely

godly (as the Earl of Essex called him), without sacri-
ficing the grace of life or the urbanities of culture.

His education was in a true sense liberal. The new
learning of the Italian Renaissance had recently taken
root in England, and the methods of the humanists were
being applied with enthusiasm in our public schools.
Ancient literature, including the philosophers and historians of Athens, formed the staple of a young man's
intellectual training. Yet no class at once so frivolous
and pedantic, so servile and so vicious, as the Italian
humanists, monopolised the art of teaching. Roger
Ascham, the tutor of princes; Sir John Cheke, at Cambridge; Camden, at Westminster; Thomas Ashton, at
Shrewsbury, were men from whom nothing but sound
learning and good morals could be imbibed. England
enjoyed the rare advantage of receiving both Renaissance
and Reformation at the same epoch. The new learning
came to our shores under the garb of Erasmus rather
than Filelfo. It was penetrated with sober piety and
enlightened philosophy instead of idle scepticism and
academical rhetoric. Thus the foundations of Sidney's
culture were broadly laid; and he was enabled to build
a substantial superstructure on them. No better companion of his early manhood could have been found than
Languet, who combined the refinements of southern with
the robust vigour of northern scholarship. The acquisition
of French, Italian, Dutch, and Spanish led him to compare modern authors with the classics; while his travels
through Europe brought him acquainted with various
manners and with the leading men of several parties.
An education so complete and many-sided polished
Sidney's excellent natural parts, until he shone the

mirror of accomplished gentlehood. He never forgot
that, in his case, studies had to be pursued, not as an
end in themselves, but as the means of fitting him for
a public career. Diligent as he was in the pursuit of
knowledge, he did not suffer himself to become a book-
worm. Athletic exercises received as much of his
attention as poetry or logic. Converse with men seemed
to him more important than communion with authors in
their printed works. In a word, he realised the ideal of
Castiglione's courtier, and personified Plato's Euphues,
in whom music was to balance gymnastic.

His breeding was that of a Court which had assumed
the polish of Italy and France, and with that polish
some of their vices and affectations. Yet the Court of
Elizabeth was, in the main, free from such corruption as
disgraced that of the Valois, and from such crimes as
shed a sinister light upon the society of Florence or
Ferrara. It was purer and more manly than the Court
of James I., and even that remained superior to the
immoralities and effeminacies of southern capitals. The
queen, with all her faults, maintained a high standard
among her servants. They represented the aristocracy
of a whole and puissant nation, united by common
patriotism and inspired by enthusiasm for their sovereign.
Conflicting religious sympathies and discordant political
theories might divide them ; but in the hour of danger,
they served their country alike, as was shown on the
great day of the Spanish Armada.

Loyalty, at that epoch, still retained the sense of
personal duty. The mediæval conviction that national
well-being depended on maintaining a hierarchy of classes,
bound together by reciprocal obligations and ascending

privileges, and presided over by a monarch who claimed
the allegiance of all, had not broken down in England.
This loyalty, like Protestant piety, was braced by the
peculiar dangers of the State, and by the special perils to
which the life of a virgin queen was now exposed. It
had little in common with decrepit affection for a dynasty,
or with such homage as nobles paid their prince in the
Italian despotisms. It was fed by the belief that the
commonwealth demanded monarchy for its support. The
Stuarts had not yet brought the name of loyalty into
contempt; and at the same time this virtue, losing its
feudal rigidity, assumed something of romantic grace and
poetic sentiment. England was personified by the lady
on the throne.

In his statesmanship, Sidney displayed the independent
spirit of a well-born Englishman, controlled by loyalty
as we have just described it. He was equally removed
from servility to his sovereign, and from the underhand
subtleties of a would-be Machiavelli. In serving the
queen he sought to serve the State. His Epistle on the
French Match, and his Defence of Sir Henry Sidney's
Irish Administration, revealed a candour rare among
Elizabeth's courtiers. With regard to England's policy
in Europe, he declared for a bold, and possibly a too
Quixotic interference in foreign affairs. Surveying the
struggle between Catholicism and Protestantism, Spanish
tyranny and national liberties, he apprehended the situation as one of extreme gravity, and was by no means
willing to temporise or trifle with it. In his young-eyed
enthusiasm, so different from Burleigh's world-worn
prudence, he desired that Elizabeth should place herself
at the head of an alliance of the Reformed Powers.

Mature experience of the home government, however, reduced these expectations; and Sidney threw himself upon a romantic but well-weighed scheme of colonisation. In each case he recommended a great policy, defined in its object, and worthy of a powerful race, to the only people whom he thought capable of carrying it out effectively.

This kindly blending of many qualities, all of them English, all of them characteristic of Elizabethan England, made Sir Philip Sidney the ideal of his generation, and for us the sweetest interpreter of its best aspirations. The essence of congruity, determining his private and his public conduct, in so many branches of active life, caused a loving nation to hail him as their Euphues. That he was not devoid of faults, faults of temper in his dealings with friends and servants, graver faults perhaps in his love for Stella, adds to the reality of his character. Shelley was hardly justified in calling him "Sublimely mild, a spirit without spot." During those last hours upon his death-bed at Arnheim, he felt that much in his past life had been but vanity, that some things in it called for repentance. But the evil inseparable from humanity was conquered long before the end. Few spirits so blameless, few so thoroughly prepared to enter upon new spheres of activity and discipline, have left this earth. The multitudes who knew him personally, those who might have been jealous of him, and those who owed him gratitude, swelled one chorus in praise of his natural goodness, his intellectual strength and moral beauty. We who study his biography, and dwell upon their testimony to his charm, derive from Sidney the noblest lesson bequeathed by Elizabethan to Vic-

torian England. It is a lesson which can never lose its
value for Greater Britain also, and for that confederated
empire which shall, if fate defeat not the high aspirations of the Anglo-Saxon race, arise to be the grandest
birth of future time.

INDEX.

Alençon, Duke of (suitor to Queen Elizabeth), 22, 23, 26
Alexander the Great, 165
Alexis, eclogue of, 78
Alps, 28, 32
America (New World), 108-109, 172-173, 176
American colonisation, 171
Amyot, Jacques, 31
Anjou, Duke of (suitor to Queen Elizabeth), 64, 66, 71, 72, 73, 104, 107, 120, 171
Antwerp, 103, 107
Arcadia, 4, 16, 80-81, 82, 87, 89, 90, 91, 103, 118, 135, 155, 185
Areopagus, 79-80, 91
Armada, 171, 197
Arnheim, 183, 199
Arthur (King), 165
Arundel (Earl of), 105
Ascham, Roger, 29, 30, 78, 196
Ashton, Thomas, 196
Astrophel (Spenser's), 190
Astrophel and Stella (sonnets), 76, 94, 95, 96, 107, 115-154
Aubrey, John, 31, 169
Audley End, 77
Axel, 180

'Basilius' (Prince of Arcadia), 86-87
Bathori, Stephen, 47
Beauchamp (House of), 6
Belarius, 183

Berkeley, Lord Thomas, 6 ; House of, 6
Blount, Sir Charles (Lord Mount-joy), 97, 122
Bourbon, Francis of, 105
Brabant, Duke of, 107
Brandon, Sir W., 4
Brill, 174
Brooke, Lord, 12, 169
Bruno, Giordano, 17, 27, 42, 170
Brysket, Lewis, 28
Burleigh, Lord, 21, 25, 36, 96, 175, 198
Butlers' war, 20
Byron, Lord, 5

Cambridge, 17, 77, 188, 196
Camden, 3, 65, 189, 196
Casimir, John, 38, 39, 60, 61
Castle of Perfect Beauty, 105, 120
Catherine de' Medici, 22, 64
Cecil, Anne, 19
Cecil (Lord Burleigh), 36
'Cecropia,' 88
Charles I., 88-89
Charles IX., 22, 23
Chartley Castle, 34
Cheke, Sir John, 196
Christ Church (Oxford), 16, 17, 19
Clanricarde, Lord, 114
'Clorinda,' 191
Coligny, 24-25

Collins's *Sidney Papers*, 185
Cologne, 43
Company of Jesus, the, 171, 195
Coningsby, Thomas, 28, 29, 53
Constable, 3, 150, 190
Council of Trent, 195
Counter Reformation, 40, 171
Court (Elizabethan), 18, 20, 25, 33, 34, 45, 48, 52, 54, 66, 70, 79, 97, 102, 177, 178, 179, 187, 197
Crashaw, Richard, 122
Crison Claudio, 100

'Dametas,' 86
Defence of Poesy, The, 32, 102, 155, 168
Dekker's plays, 59
De l'Isle, Edmund, Viscount, 5
De l'Isle (family of), 6
'Desire and Love' (sonnets), 153
Deventer, 181
Devereux, Lady Penelope, 34-35, 37, 96, 97, 115-132
Devereux, Robert, Earl of Essex, 114
Devonshire, Countess of, 97
Devonshire, Earl of, 97
Diana (Constable's), 150
Diana (Montemayor's), 82
Discovery of the Gaping Gulf, The, (Stubbs's), 64
Don Antonio, 107, 177
Doncaster, Viscount, 69
Don John of Austria, 43
'Dorus,' 86-87
Drake, Sir Francis, 42, 108, 176, 177, 178, 195
Drummond, 32
Dudley, Edmund, 6
Dudley, Sir John, 6
Dudley, Lady Mary (mother to Sidney), 5, 13
Dudley, House of, 7, 174
Durham House, 34
Du Simiers, 64-65
Dyer, Edward, 17, 62, 79, 107

Earl, Dr., 89

Edward de Vere (Earl of Oxford), 19
Edward VI., 5
Edward IV., 140
Eikon Basiliké, 89
Elector Palatine, 38
Elector Lewis, 39
Elizabeth (Queen), 10, 20, 22, 23, 25, 34, 38, 44, 47, 50, 54, 59, 60, 61, 64-67, 102, 103-104, 108-110, 171, 173, 174, 179, 180, 186, 193, 197, 198, 199
Elizabeth (daughter of Baron De L'Isle), 6
Empson, Sir Richard, 6
Essex, Earl of, 34-35, 36, 37, 96, 196
Essex, Lady (wife of Earl of Leicester), 36, 65
Etienne, Henri, 169
'Euphues,' 3, 197
Euphues (Lyly's), 82, 90

Ferdinand, Emperor, 39
Fitz-William, Sir W., 5, 21
Flanders, 43, 174
Flushing, 174, 179, 186
Fœdus Evangelicum, 40, 48
Fortress of Perfect Beauty, 105
'Fortunatus,' 59
'Four Foster Children of Desire,' 105
France, 22
Francis of Bourbon, 105
Frankfort, 26, 27, 32
French Court, 24, 105
French Crown, 22, 24, 73, 104, 174
Frobisher's expedition, 45, 108
Fulke Greville, 3, 11, 12, 17, 21, 23, 28, 31, 37, 38, 40, 43, 44, 62, 65, 67, 70, 77, 79, 105, 107, 155, 170, 171, 172, 175, 176, 177, 184, 185, 187, 188
Fuller, 3, 29, 47

Genoa, 32
German Powers, 38, 40
Gifford, George, 183, 184, 187
Gilbert, Sir Humphrey, 108, 109

Gli Eroici Furori (Giordano Bruno's), 170

Gorboduc, 80, 167, 169

Gosson, Stephen (author of *The School of Abuse*), 156

Greek Testament, Henri Etienne's edition of, 169

Greene, Robert, 29, 78, 90, 167

Greenwich, 44

Grey, Lady Elizabeth, 6, 140

Grey, Elizabeth, 6

Grey, Lady Jane, 192

Grey, Lord (of Wilton), 95

Grey, Sir Edward, 6

Grosart, Dr., 153

Gruitthueisens, Madame, 183

Guarini, 57

Guise, Duke of, 24, 25

'Gynecia,' 86, 87

Hakluyt, Richard, 108, 169

Hampton Court, 56

Hapsburg, Rudolph of, 38, 39

Harrington, Sir James, 4

Harvey, Gabriel, 29, 43, 77 *seq.*

Hay, James (Viscount Doncaster), 69

Heidelberg, 26, 32, 39, 43

Henri III., 47, 64, 104

Henry VIII., 4, 5, 41

Herbert, William, Earl of Pembroke (Sidney's nephew), 95

Herodotus, 157

Hohenlohe, Count, 180

Hollingshed, Chronicle of, 5, 53

Huguenots, 22, 23, 24-25, 42, 171

Huntingdon, Earl of, 96, 111

'Indian project,' 45, 108

Ireland, 10, 11, 18, 20, 34, 48-51, 56

Italian Renaissance, 196

James I., 97

Jesuits, 173

Johnson, Dr., 89

Jonson, Ben, 3, 8, 9, 11, 32, 38, 76, 77, 85, 100

Juxon, Bishop, 88-89

Kenilworth Castle, 34

La Cena delle Ceneri (Bruno's dialogue), 170

La Cuisse Rompue, 183

Lady of the May, The, 54

Lamb, Charles, 123

Lane, Ralph, 175

Languet, Hubert, 27, 28, 30, 31, 32, 36, 37, 39, 43, 45-46, 47, 55, 61-62, 66, 102, 103, 196

Leicester, Earl of, 6, 7, 18, 19, 23, 25, 28, 34, 36, 54, 65, 66, 97, 98, 173, 178, 179, 181, 183, 186 187

Leicester, Edmund, Earl of, 174

Leicester's Commonwealth, 173

Leicester House, 100, 141

Lewis William of Nassau, 181

Life and Death of Sir Philip Sidney, The, by Philophilippus, 16, 47, 135, 187

Life of Sidney, by Dr. Zouch, 169

Life of Sidney, by Fulke Greville, 172

Lincoln, Earl of, 23

L'Isle, Viscount, 69

Lo Spaccio della Bestia Trionfante (Giordano Bruno's), 170

Loyola, Ignatius, 195

Ludlow Castle, 22, 179

Lyly, John, 77, 82, 167

Madox, Griffin, 28

Margaret (sister to Charles IX.), 22, 23, 24, 26

Marino, 57, 126

Mary, Queen of England, 7-8, 195

Massacre of St. Bartholomew, 24-25, 27, 195

Maurice, Count, of Nassau, 178

Maximilian, Emperor, 32

Melanchthon, 27

Mendoza, 186

Milton, 86, 87, 89

Mirror of Magistrates, 166, 169

'Miso,' 86

Molineux, Edward, 5, 52-53, 56

Montagu (House of), 4

Montemayor, 82
'Mopsa,' 86
Mornay, Philip du Plessis, 103, 186
Mort d'Arthur, 194
Mountjoy, Lord (Sir Charles Blount), 97
'Musidorus, Prince of Thessalia,' 83-87

Nash, Thomas, 119, 152, 189
Naunton, Sir Robert, 47
Navarre, Henry of, 22, 23
Netherlands, 42, 43, 61, 172, 174, 178, 186
Newman, T. (printer of first edition of *Astrophel and Stella*, 1591), 117-118
New World, the, 108, 173, 174
Noel (family of), 4
Norris, Sir John, 181
North America, grant of land to Sidney in, 109
North (family of), 4
Northumberland, Duke of, 6, 7
Norton, 77

Ormond, Earl of, 20, 36, 48
Oxford, 16-18, 188
Oxford, Earl of, 19, 30, 65-68

Page, 65
Paris, 23, 24-25, 64, 105, 195
Parliament, Sidney in, 104
Parma, Duke of, 181
Peckham, Sir George, 108, 110
Pembroke, Countess of, 3, 76, 118, 191
Pembroke, Earl of, 7, 48, 51
Penshurst, 4, 7, 8-9, 85
'Phillisides,' 94, 103, 107
'Philoclea,' 86, 88
Philophilippus (author of *Life and Death of Sir Philip Sidney*), 16
Plato, 157, 165
Polish Crown, Sidney's candidature for the, 47
Protestant League, 42, 172
Psalms of David, Sidney's renderings of the, 76

Pugliano, 32
'Pyrocles, Prince of Macedon,' 83, 87

Raleigh, 108, 173, 190, 195
Rammekins, Castle of, 174, 178
Ratcliffe, Thomas, Earl of Sussex, 5
Renaissance, 2, 77, 193, 196
Rich, Lady (Lady Penelope Devereux), 96-97, 116
Rich, Lord, 37, 96, 97, 115
'Rombus,' 54-55
Roydon, Matthew, 190
Ruins of Time (Spenser's), 190
Rutland, Countess of, 178

Sannazzaro, 82, 90
School of Abuse, The (Gosson's), 156
Shakespeare, 77, 95, 116, 131, 150, 153, 167
Shelley, 1, 159, 191, 199
Shepherd's Kalendar, The (Spenser's), 79, 166, 169
Shrewsbury, 11, 13, 196
Sidney, Ambrozia (sister), 33
Sidney, Lady Dorothea, 9
Sidney, Elizabeth (daughter), afterwards Countess of Rutland, 178
Sidney, Frances (wife), 110, 114, 153, 179, 183
Sidney, Mary (sister), 7, 13, 48, 80
Sidney, Lady Mary (mother), 7, 15-16, 21-22, 36, 51, 53, 56, 61, 113-114
Sidney, Sir Henry (father), 5, 7, 10, 11, 13, 15, 18, 20, 21, 22, 23, 26, 35, 36, 44, 48, 53, 60, 61, 102, 108, 110-114, 179, 180, 187, 198
Sidney, Nicholas, 4
Sidney Papers (Collins's), 185
Sidney, Sir Philip. The beauty of his character, 1-4 ; his ancestry, 4 - 7 ; his birth, 7 ; sent to school at Shrewsbury, 11 ; goes into residence at Christ Church, Oxford, 16 ; taken under pro-

tection of the Earl of Leicester, 18 ; goes on "The Grand Tour," 23 ; appointed Gentleman in Ordinary of the bedchamber of Charles IX., 24 ; return to England, 32 ; entry into Court life, 34 ; visit to Ireland, 34 ; sent by Queen Elizabeth to Germany, 38 ; and to the Netherlands, 43 ; returns to London, 44 ; leaves the Court, 70 ; *Arcadia* begun at Wilton, 80 ; enters Parliament for Kent, 104 ; his marriage, 110 ; *Astrophel and Stella* composed, 116 ; *The Defence of Poesy*, 156 ; in the House of Commons, 173 ; leaves England for the Low Countries, 178 ; death, 186 ; burial in St. Paul's, 186

Sidney, Sir Robert (brother), 10, 98-102, 108, 183, 185

Sidney, Sir Thomas (brother), 183

Sidney Sussex College, 5

Spenser, 58, 76, 79, 95, 156, 169, 190-191

Stella (Lady Penelope Devereux), 97, 107, 116, 153, 199

St. Bartholomew, Massacre of, 24, 25, 27, 195

St. Paul's Cathedral, Sidney's burial in, 186

Strasburg, 26, 32

Stubbs, 65

Surrey, Lord, 77, 166, 169

Tasso, 57, 82, 158

Thornton, Dr Thomas (Dean of Christ Church), 17

United Provinces, 174, 179

Valentinian (Fletcher's), 59

Venice, 31, 32

Veronese, Paolo, portrait of Sidney by, 31

Vienna, 28, 32

Virginia, 173, 175

Walpole, Horace, 83, 174

Walsingham, Francis, 22, 23, 26, 28, 44, 61, 102, 104, 179, 180, 182, 183, 186-187

Wanstead, 54

Waterhouse, Edward, 35, 50

West Indies, 172, 176

Wier, John, 184

William the Silent (Prince of Orange), 43, 44, 103, 104, 107, 171, 178

Wilton, 17, 48, 70, 76, 80, 82, 95

'Zelmane,' 86-88

Zouch, Dr., 55, 90, 169

Zutphen, 181, 182

THE END

Printed by R. & R. CLARK, LIMITED, *Edinburgh*.

English Men of Letters.

Edited by JOHN MORLEY.

Popular Edition.   Crown 8vo.   Paper Covers, 1s.; *Cloth,* 1s. 6d. *each.*
Library Edition.   Crown 8vo.   Gilt tops.   Flat backs. 2s. *net each.*

ADDISON. By W. J. COURTHOPE.
BACON. By Dean CHURCH.
BENTLEY. By Sir RICHARD JEBB.
BUNYAN. By J. A. FROUDE.
BURKE. By JOHN MORLEY.
BURNS. By Principal SHAIRP.
BYRON. By Professor NICHOL.
CARLYLE. By Professor NICHOL.
CHAUCER. By Dr. A. W. WARD.
COLERIDGE. By H. D. TRAILL.
COWPER. By GOLDWIN SMITH.
DEFOE. By W. MINTO.
DE QUINCEY. By Prof. MASSON.
DICKENS. By Dr. A. W. WARD.
DRYDEN. By Prof. SAINTSBURY.
FIELDING. By AUSTIN DOBSON.
GIBBON. By J. C. MORISON.
GOLDSMITH. By W. BLACK.
GRAY. By EDMUND GOSSE.
HAWTHORNE. By HENRY JAMES.
HUME. By Prof. HUXLEY, F.R.S.
JOHNSON. By Sir LESLIE STEPHEN, K.C.B.

KEATS. By SIDNEY COLVIN.
LAMB, CHARLES. By Canon AINGER.
LANDOR. By SIDNEY COLVIN.
LOCKE. By THOMAS FOWLER.
MACAULAY. By J. C. MORISON.
MILTON. By MARK PATTISON.
POPE. By Sir LESLIE STEPHEN, K.C.B.
SCOTT. By R. H. HUTTON.
SHELLEY. By J. A. SYMONDS.
SHERIDAN. By Mrs. OLIPHANT.
SIDNEY. By J. A. SYMONDS.
SOUTHEY. By Prof. DOWDEN.
SPENSER. By Dean CHURCH.
STERNE. By H. D. TRAILL.
SWIFT. By Sir LESLIE STEPHEN, K.C.B.
THACKERAY. By ANTHONY TROLLOPE.
WORDSWORTH. By F. W. H. MYERS.

NEW SERIES.

Crown 8vo.   Gilt tops.   Flat backs. 2s. *net each.*

GEORGE ELIOT. By Sir LESLIE STEPHEN, K.C.B.
HAZLITT. By AUGUSTINE BIRRELL, K.C.
MATTHEW ARNOLD. By HERBERT W. PAUL.
RUSKIN. By FREDERIC HARRISON.
TENNYSON. By Sir ALFRED LYALL.
RICHARDSON. By AUSTIN DOBSON.
BROWNING. By G. K. CHESTERTON.
CRABBE. By ALFRED AINGER.
FANNY BURNEY. By AUSTIN DOBSON.
JEREMY TAYLOR. By EDMUND GOSSE.
ROSSETTI. By A. C. BENSON.
MARIA EDGEWORTH. By the Hon. EMILY LAWLESS.
HOBBES. By Sir LESLIE STEPHEN, K.C.B.
ADAM SMITH. By FRANCIS W. HIRST.

THOMAS MOORE. By STEPHEN GWYNN.
SYDNEY SMITH. By GEORGE W. E. RUSSELL.
EDWARD FITZGERALD. By A. C. BENSON.
ANDREW MARVELL. By AUGUSTINE BIRRELL, K.C.
SIR THOMAS BROWNE. By EDMUND GOSSE.
WALTER PATER. By ARTHUR C. BENSON.
MRS. GASKELL. By CLEMENT SHORTER.
CHARLES KINGSLEY. By G. K. CHESTERTON.
SHAKESPEARE. By WALTER RALEIGH.
JAMES THOMSON. By G. C. MACAULAY.

MACMILLAN AND CO., LTD., LONDON.

English Men of Action Series.

Crown 8vo.　Cloth.　With Portraits.　2s. 6d. each.

CAMPBELL (COLIN).
By ARCHIBALD FORBES.
CLIVE.
By Sir CHARLES WILSON.
COOK (Captain).
By Sir WALTER BESANT.
DAMPIER.
By W. CLARK RUSSELL.
DRAKE.
By JULIAN CORBETT.
DUNDONALD.
By the Hon. J. W. FORTESCUE.
GORDON (General).
By Sir W. BUTLER.
HASTINGS (Warren).
By Sir A. LYALL.
HAVELOCK (Sir Henry).
By A. FORBES.
HENRY V.
By the Rev. A. J. CHURCH.
LAWRENCE (Lord).
By Sir RICHARD TEMPLE.

LIVINGSTONE.
By THOMAS HUGHES.
MONK.
By JULIAN CORBETT.
MONTROSE.
By MOWBRAY MORRIS.
NAPIER (Sir Charles).
By Colonel Sir W. BUTLER.
NELSON.
By Prof. J. K. LAUGHTON.
PETERBOROUGH.
By W. STEBBING.
RODNEY.
By DAVID HANNAY.
STRAFFORD.
By H. D. TRAILL.
WARWICK, the King-Maker.
By C. W. OMAN.
WELLINGTON.
By GEORGE HOOPER.
WOLFE.
By A. G. BRADLEY.

Twelve English Statesmen.

Crown 8vo.　2s. 6d. each.

** *A Series of Short Biographies, not designed to be a complete roll of famous Statesmen, but to present in historic order the lives and work of those leading actors in our affairs who by their direct influence have left an abiding mark on the policy, the institutions, and the position of Great Britain among States.*

WILLIAM THE CON-QUEROR. By EDWARD A. FREE-MAN, D.C.L., LL.D., late Regius Professor of Modern History in the University of Oxford.
HENRY II.
By Mrs. J. R. GREEN.
EDWARD I.
By T. F. TOUT, M.A., Professor of History, The Owens College, Manchester.
HENRY VII.
By JAMES GAIRDNER.
CARDINAL WOLSEY.
By Bishop CREIGHTON, D.D., late Dixie Professor of Ecclesiastical History in the University of Cambridge.

ELIZABETH.
By E. S. BEESLY, M.A., Professor of Modern History, University College, London.
OLIVER CROMWELL.
By FREDERIC HARRISON.
WILLIAM III.
By H. D. TRAILL.
WALPOLE.
By JOHN MORLEY.
CHATHAM.
By JOHN MORLEY. [*In preparation*
PITT.
By Lord ROSEBERY.
PEEL.
By J. R. THURSFIELD, M.A. late Fellow of Jesus College, Oxford.

MACMILLAN AND CO., LTD., LONDON.